Fair and Just

By

Cé MacCiaran

ISBN: 0-7596-7413-2

This book is printed on acid free paper.

1stBooks - rev. 1/09/02

Chapter One

It was late afternoon when Ky Gearan entered the dayroom. Indifferent housekeeping, dust was everywhere. It was Sunday, and the cleaning staff had the weekend off. Sundays after lunch were free time for the patients in the addiction unit. Ky sat down on the worn green leather couch, but he was facing the sun, and soon moved to a chair behind the pool table. The sun had faded the felt cover of the pool table from green to tan in spots. He looked at the rack of balls on the table. The eight ball was missing.

A ping-pong table to Ky's right was missing a net. There were a few books on the shelf near the door, and some tattered magazines on the table next to it. Looking out of the window on the left, Ky saw the brown hills beyond - tinder for brush fires. The California weather seemed the same, not a drop of rain, and 80's and 90's every day. Ky didn't care for Los Angeles in July. Only daily watering had kept the hospital grounds green.

Some of the other patients had gathered in the TV lounge next door for the Dodgers and Braves game that was about to start. "Come on over and watch it with us," said Robin."

"No, thank you, I'm not much of a fan." Ky had neither patience nor interest to watch sports on the tube. He wondered if this was one reason he had few men friends. Robin was Ky's roommate. Today, he had slept in until nearly noon. Robin was about six feet tall, heavyset, with unruly reddish brown hair. Two days' stubble graced his chin. Ky had been rousting him at ten minutes before nine during the week, so they could attend group therapy.

Ky heard crowd noises next door. Guess the Dodgers have scored a run? He wondered again if he should join the others. Maybe this would take his mind off "Family Week," which was beginning the next day. When Ky was admitted to Del Cara Hospital, he had to sign an agreement to invite his wife and family to this week's program. Hell, he would have signed anything, being in a state of near-collapse.

He'd been dreading Gwyn's and Jason's visit since his arrival three weeks ago. He wondered if they were now landing at LA International. Gwyn had been able to get an emergency judge to fill in for her in court this week. Most of all, he dreaded what she would say tomorrow. He had sensed a change in her mood when she called on Wednesday. She had hung up without telling him that she loved him.

Ky was glad that Jason, his eldest, had agreed to come. He knew that Jason's wife, Dana, had not wanted him to visit, as she had never liked Ky and had written him off since the publicity appeared. Jason would be a source of strength for Ky. He resembled his father - blond hair and fair skin with blue eyes - although he was two inches taller. Ky had never made six feet; Jason topped that by an inch.

Ky began to think about what he would say to Gwyn. He knew that he would have to tell her everything. He knew that there was no other way now. Ky took out the birthday card that Fiona, his youngest daughter, had sent him. He had been carrying it in his pocket for more than a week. She always knew what to say and do. He was grateful that she and her husband, Ken, had traveled cross-country with him to the hospital. Was it now just over a year that she and Ken had been married?

He thought again about the day of her wedding. How could he ever forget it? Ky had spent that hot afternoon in June standing near the kitchen window of his home, making call after call, in a vain attempt to find Verna, who had not delivered the bridesmaids dresses for Fiona's wedding. Was this the day that set in motion all the events that led him to this place? Ky knew better.

They had begun well before that day. It was when he met Verna, a state probation officer. Now, standing in the dayroom of the hospital, Ky remembered her telephone call one chilly February day last year.

"Hello, Mr. Gearan, I'm Verna Evans. I supervise Willie Jackson, one of your clients. I've just learned that the judge has set his hearing for tomorrow. Could you meet me in the bailiff's lounge at the morning break?" Ky handed a file to his secretary and replied, "Yes, I'll be glad to. I'm in court for another case."

There were no lawyer conference rooms at the courthouse. It was customary to meet probation and parole officers in the lounge. Lawyers had to speak to their clients in the halls outside the courtrooms. A few minutes before ten, he walked up Freedom Street, to the courthouse. The lounge was on the third floor, behind Courtroom 3A, where the hearing would be held before Judge Brenda Moore.

Just before the break, Ky entered the lounge. He noticed the worn, stained gray tweed upholstery and smelled a blend of tobacco and coffee. Smoking was not permitted in the lobbies and halls. The lounge was the only place for bailiffs and lawyers to grab a quick smoke and a cup of coffee. Ky wondered why the state couldn't afford to buy new furniture. Gwyn's office wasn't much better. Only the Chief Judge had new furniture. The Chief Judge's political party controlled the legislature, and the party would see that their officeholders got the perks. Ky saw two bailiffs smoking near the door. To the rear of the lounge, he saw a slender, blonde woman in her late thirties or early forties, who was drinking coffee. She wore tiny granny glasses perched near the end of her nose and a blue suit that flattered her figure.

Ky drew a cup of coffee from the urn and went over to her. She rose to greet him. "I'm Verna. I transferred here last month from Gaston."

"Glad to meet you. I wondered who had been given the supervision of my client."

Ky had heard the rumors that had been circulating around the courthouse about the newly transferred probation officer. Allegedly, the person had had an affair with an assistant district attorney that led to the breakup of his marriage and had led to her transfer from Glaston to the Dual Cities. He generally

3

discounted all such rumors. "Verna, how long have you been a probation officer?" He put a dollar in the can next to the urn for donations to the coffee fund. Verna put down her coffee cup and lit a cigarette.

"I'm starting my seventeenth year," she said. "I come from a 'state' family. My dad was a corrections officer, and my mother has just retired as director of the Detention Center for Juveniles in Richland County."

Ky took a sip of coffee, which was strong enough to float an axe head. Some things never change. "Verna, I've had a few clients that have spent time in the Richland County unit."

"I bet my mother knew them. She called all of them by their first name. Now, Mr. Gearan, what do you want me to do with your client? Revoke him or continue his probation?"

Ky was startled by the offer. Not a usual attitude for a probation officer, but he recovered quickly. "I really think my client deserves another chance. He now has a job, has enrolled in a drug outpatient treatment program, is catching up on his child support, and is making payment on his court fine and victim restitution. There has been a definite improvement in his attitude over the past few months."

"Okay, Mr. Gearan, I'll recommend that he be continued on probation."

"It sounds like the break is over, Verna. Let's go into the courtroom."

The judge followed Verna's recommendation and allowed Ky's client to stay on probation. Ky continued the other case he had because a witness failed to appear. On the way back to his office, Ky thought about Verna's easy compliance. Was it because she knew Gwyn was a judge and sought to curry favor? He had an uneasy feeling about this.

Soon Ky noticed that Verna began coming by Gwyn's office during morning or afternoon breaks. Verna shared choice bits of courthouse gossip. One day Verna dropped by while Ky was there to ask Gwyn to lunch. "Good afternoon Judge, and Mr. Gearan. How are you fine folks today?"

Okay," Ky replied.

Gwyn said, "Very fine, and you?"

"Tolerable, Judge, tolerable."

"Verna, you sew, don't you?" Gwyn asked.

"Yes, Judge. I did the dresses for Ron Taub's wedding. Their theme was "black and white."

"Ky and I went to the wedding, and we were impressed by the dresses. I don't think we had ever seen a father and a stepfather give the bride away. Would you consider doing the dresses for our daughter Fiona? Her wedding is the last Saturday in June."

"Yes, Judge, I would be glad to and, if you like, I'll do the little flower-girl dresses, also."

That evening, Fiona dropped in on Ky and Gwyn. She was wearing her long blonde hair in a ponytail and sporting a blue sweater and plaid skirt.

"Fiona, I've got someone at the courthouse to do the bridesmaids' dresses."

"Okay, mom. I don't really know anyone else who can do them."

The next day, Fiona bought expensive silk material in varying shades of pink. Ky delivered the material to Verna on Saturday. Verna lived in a small, two-bedroom house on the East Side. He knew the neighborhood. It was a couple of blocks from a house Ky had lived in as a boy.

Ky knocked and Verna quickly answered. "Come in, Mr. Gearan. I see you have the material. Did you bring the patterns?"

"I'll get them from the car," Ky said.

"Tell the judge not to worry. I'll have them ready at least a week before the wedding."

Ky noticed a large, white dog penned in her backyard. He thought it strange that the dog hadn't barked. When he returned home, he told Gwyn and Fiona that he had delivered the material. They seemed pleased, but he wondered why he still felt uneasy.

Soon Verna began to drop by their home on occasion. She asked few questions about the dresses and said little about her progress on them. She admired the couple's French antiques, Oriental carpets, and modern art. She frequently praised Ky and Gwyn for their tolerant and friendly manner.

"Judge and Mr. Gearan, it would be great if everyone were like you." Verna commented. "Judge, I'm telling all my friends to vote for you in your election next year. I can't work for you directly, but I can get many of my friends to spread the word and help out."

"Thanks, Verna. I'm sure there will be strong opposition in the race."

Ky thought Verna was laying on the flattery a bit thick. This fed his sense of unease. Gwyn called Verna about the dresses a couple of weeks before the wedding.

"Don't you worry, judge," she replied. "They'll be ready when I told you they would."

The Saturday before the wedding came and went. No dresses had been delivered. The day of the wedding came, still no Verna, still no dresses. Ky stood by the kitchen window, calling every few minutes. Then he thought to call Verna's supervisor.

"Mary Lou? Ky Gearan. I've been trying to reach Verna all afternoon, but she doesn't answer. Don't you live in her neighborhood? You do? Would you mind driving by her house and checking on her?

"I'll be glad to, Mr. Gearan. It's only a couple of blocks."

In a few minutes, she called back. "The door's locked, and her car and dog are gone."

Gwyn called Ky a few minutes before six. "Hurry, you have to give the bride away at six."

Ky quickly adjusted his Dress Donald kilt, put on his "Prince Charlie" coat and vest, and sped to his sister Linda's farm for the wedding. At six, he was at Linda's front door. No Verna, and no dresses. Gwyn shouted, "Where's Verna! Where are the dresses?"

Fiona was sobbing and Elena, her matron of honor, was furious. "Dad, what are we going to do? Everyone is waiting. What'll we do?"

About twenty after six, Verna drove up, dumped the dresses in the foyer, and drove away without a word. The dresses were in a shambles, barely tacked together. Gwyn, Linda and Dana had to sew the dresses on the bridesmaids. All prayed that they would hold together for the wedding.

It had been raining. The wedding guests were huddled in the refreshment tent. The bridesmaids came down the stairs, just as the rain was ending. The guests followed the wedding party to the outdoor chapel next to the lake.

Ky proudly led Fiona on his arm to the rear of the chapel. A string quartet was playing "Pachelbel's Canon." They paused, awaiting the wedding march. Ky saw Ken, the groom, and his father, at the right of the altar, clad in white dinner jackets. Fiona's Uncle Rob, a retired minister, was wearing his clerical garb.

Ky escorted Fiona to the altar. Uncle Rob asked, "Who gives this woman in marriage?"

"Her mother and I," Ky said.

The couple repeated their vows. Uncle Rob said, "You may kiss your bride!"

At this moment, Ky felt as if he were floating off the ground. He shed tears of joy, as did Gwyn.

A Celtic harper and fiddler played for the wedding reception. Ky had also offered to pay a piper to play at the wedding. "No, dad, not at my wedding," Fiona had said. "But you may wear your clan Donald Dress kilt."

After the reception, the cake cutting, and the tossing of the bride's bouquet, the dancing began. Fiona had arranged for two bands. They young folks danced to a rock bank from Kilmont, while Gwyn, Ky and some of the more senior guests found the rhythms of Gil Galbraith's "Golden Oldie" band more to their liking. While dancing, Ky had the sensation of gliding over the

7

dance floor. Fiona made his joy complete, by having the last dance with him.

The last guests left the farm around midnight. Fiona and Ken had left for an unknown destination, before flying to Jamaica the next day. Weary and happy, Gwyn and Ky got into their car and drove through the woods at Linda's farm and onto the highway. There were few cars on the road and soon they were home.

"Ky, I never thought that we would get to this day."

"Neither did I, Gwyn, neither did I."

Chapter Two

A couple of weeks after Fiona's wedding, Ky was at his desk in the Old Fire House. The building had been erected by the Village of Brethren. The village merged with the Dual Cities some sixty years earlier. Ky bought a one-half interest in the restored building when he was terminated as house counsel for the trucking company after twenty years. Built at the end of the 19th century, it was made of brick produced by a former slave. The architect had combined entrances covered by "Brethren Bonnets," semicircular hoods, with an Italianate square bell tower reminiscent of those found in Sienna. It was eclectic, but tasteful. Inside, the floors were heart of pine and the thick masonry walls were plastered.

Gwyn had helped Ky decorate his offices. She chose a Kurdish prayer rug in a dusky rose hue, off-white sofa, French-style desk, Queen Anne desk chair, brown leather side chair, and red antique Korean chest. Behind the desk was a square panel in the floor - a cover for the hole that used to accommodate firemen as they slid down the brass pole to the engine below. Many a time, when faced with a difficult client, Ky wished it were still there

Ky had begun looking at a file when Fiona burst in. She was red-faced and trembling. "Dad, I want you to sue the bitch! Sue Verna! I can't use those dresses for anything at all. All that silk material was wasted."

"Close the door, Fiona. We need to discuss this thoroughly."

"I know, dad, but I am out more than nine hundred dollars for the material, and it is worthless now."

"Before we get started, how was your trip to Jamaica?"

Fiona had returned early that morning from her honeymoon. She looked lovely, clad in a white linen sundress that showed off her golden tan and golden curls. She glowed with beauty. Ky envied her tan. Fiona had taken after Gwyn, not after him, with his pale Scotch complexion covered with freckles. Gwyn could

9

tan, because of her Welsh ancestry, and she had light brown hair, lively brown eyes and olive skin.

By now, Fiona had calmed down a bit, and she took a seat on the couch. "It was a fabulous trip, dad. We stayed at the Golden Shores, where you and mom stayed the Christmas before I was born."

"Is O'Hara O'Neil still there, and is he still the best singer on the island?"

"Yes, he saw my resemblance to mom and asked about you all. He said, 'Your mom and dad are the kindest folks; you're so lucky.'"

"Now, Fiona, about your claim against Verna. She owns no property, and a judgment against her would be worthless. No way to collect anything at all from her."

"You are right, dad, but I'm still mad and hurt. No way to use these dresses for anything. All that money is lost - not to mention my humiliation on my wedding day."

"Very well, Fiona. I'll dictate a demand letter for you."

Ky did as he had promised, but he felt he was acting against both his best judgment and also his best intuition. He squelched his temptation to tell Fiona of his fears about Verna. He did not want to douse the glow from her wedding and honeymoon. Verna replied a week later in "legalese," saying that she would pay nothing to Fiona. Ky showed the letter to his daughter, and she agreed that this would be the end of it. Ky had a gut feeling, though, that this was just the beginning for him. He felt that Verna would not let this go.

Several weeks later, Valerie, a former client of Ky's, gave him a call. She was upset.

"Mr. Gearan, Howard has left me and the twins and moved in with another woman. He left me with all the bills, and has said that he wasn't going to give me any money. What can I do?"

Valerie! Ky felt a twinge of conscience. He hoped he could handle her support case by a separation agreement. He didn't want her to come to his office. "Will Howard sign a separation agreement? What do you need per week or per month for the upkeep of the twins?"

"I don't know, Mr. Gearan, maybe he will sign. I need $100 a week for them."

"Valerie, is that enough money?"

"No, but we probably can't get him to pay that much."

"Okay. I'll draft an agreement with standard clauses and ask for $100 a week support, payable each Friday. Also, we'll provide visitation for Howard at his place on alternate weekends.

The next day, Ky drafted the agreement and mailed it to Howard. He hoped against hope that Howard would sign it. He couldn't forget what had happened that Saturday morning nearly two years ago, when Valerie had come to his office. Ky had represented Valerie on drug charges and gotten her probation. She also had hired him on worthless checks charges. She came by that day, she said, to make a payment on the fee. Ky was working on a transcript of a case that he had appealed; the brief was due the following Friday. There was a knock at the door. It was Valerie.

"Mr. Gearan, I saw your light from the street. Hope you aren't too busy. Came by to make a payment. I left the twins in the car with my stepson."

"I am a bit busy, but come on in."

She entered the office suite. Ky noticed her tight-fitting beige dress. It flattered her figure. "So you're making a payment? Let me get my receipt book."

She followed Ky into his private office. He took the receipt book out of his desk drawer. Valerie leaned across the desk holding a twenty-dollar bill. Ky could see the milky-white cleavage between her breasts and caught a faint scent of musk.

"Like what you see?" Valerie asked.

"Yes. But I'm a married man."

"Yeah, I know. You're a married to a judge."

She leaned closer - so close, she was in his face. He tried to move away, but on impulse, he embraced her and their lips met. Soon they were making love on the couch.

"Valerie, there is a ladies' room at the end of the hall on the right."

"Thanks. I'll go and clean up."

Ky went into the men's room. He felt drained and empty of emotion, all except shame. Guilt and regret soon followed. "Why? Oh, why? Why did I do this again? Why can't I be satisfied with Gwyn?"

In the hall, he ran into Valerie.

"Reckon, I'd better get back to the twins. Really enjoyed it. Hope to see you again soon."

"Valerie, we can't do this again. I don't know what came over me. Sorry that this happened."

"All right, Mr. Gearan, I understand."

Slowly, Valerie went down the steps. He watched from his office window until she drove off.

Ky returned to the transcript. He couldn't concentrate and left the office. He was glad that he didn't have to face Gwyn today. She should be at her mother's condo in Campbellton by now. Ky found a note from Gwyn when he arrived home, telling him what food there was in the refrigerator and that she would see him Sunday. She signed the note, "Love, Gwyn."

What if Gwyn were to find out? What would she do this time? Damn… Damn… Damn.

Valerie called him a week later. "Bad news, Mr. Gearan, Howard won't sign, said he won't pay me a dime. What can we do now? My paycheck is not nearly enough to take care of the twins."

"Probably. Howard needs the stimulus of a summons. You need to go to the Clerk of Court's office and sign a warrant for nonsupport."

"I'll do that today after work, Mr. Gearan. Oh, by the way, do you know my probation office, Verna?"

"Yes, why so?"

"She asked me whether I knew that you had given drugs to and had sex with clients."

"That's not true."

Ky had never taken drugs nor had he given drugs to anyone. He hadn't had a drink or even a cigarette in more than twenty years.

"Mr. Gearan, I didn't believe that drug part," Valerie said. "You have always seemed to be clean and sober. Why would Verna tell me this?"

"Valerie, I don't know why she would want to hurt my reputation by lying about this. Do you know of any others that she may have told this to?"

"No, I don't. Sorry she put the badmouth on you."

Ky wondered if Verna's lies had anything to do with Fiona and the bridesmaids' dresses. Was she incensed by the demand letter he had written? Most likely. The seeds of anxiety began to sprout in his middle.

Valerie's child support case was set for the first Monday in October. Ky felt an autumn chill from the brisk wind blowing between the buildings on Freedom Street, as he walked the two long blocks to the courthouse. The chill lingered as he went into the courtroom. The clerk called the case, but Valerie had not appeared.

"Your Honor, I move for a two weeks' continuance," Ky said. "This is the first time on for this case, and the defendant doesn't object." The assistant DA joined in the motion.

"Motion granted. The case is continued."

Two weeks later, Ky returned to the courtroom for Valerie's case. He had not been able to find her. Her telephone was disconnected. His letter was returned, "Moved, No Forwarding Address." Her employer reported that she hadn't returned to work in over a month. Valerie's stepmother didn't know where she could be. Ky had no choice but to take a voluntary dismissal of her case.

Howard was now taking care of the twins. Valerie had, in effect, abandoned them and would likely lose custody.

A few weeks later, Ky received a telephone call from Howard. "I know what you did. My preacher and me been praying over it, and it will all come out."

13

How did Howard find out? Did Valerie tell him? Who else might know about them? Did she tell Verna? An ache in the pit of his stomach began to grow and deepen.

Valerie's stepmother called Ky in mid-December. "Mr. Gearan, Valerie has been arrested on drug charges. She wants you to visit her in jail."

Ky told his secretary to cancel his afternoon appointments, and hastened to the jail. He felt uneasy on the three-block walk there. He knew that he shouldn't represent her on these charges. He needed to stay away from her.

Valerie was escorted to the conference cell. He scarcely recognized her. Her red hair was unkempt and unwashed. She was pale and emaciated. Her jumpsuit hung on her wasted frame. She had lost her figure to cocaine.

"It's a good thing that you're wearing a jumpsuit, otherwise you couldn't keep your clothes on," Ky said.

"Crack. It's the crack cocaine - don't eat nothing - don't sleep - stay up for days. Crack did this to me. I was going to call you, really I was. Started partying during State's homecoming weekend. I lost my job. I've lost my kids. I've lost everything. Please get me outta here. I'll do anything - only get me outta here."

"Valerie, I think you need another lawyer now. Mark Grant would be good to represent you in these kinds of cases."

"No, no…I need you. You know my background. You have always gotten me off before."

"Valerie, it's true, I do know your background, but I don't think I can help you this time."

He remembered reading the presentencing report in the other drug cases. The report showed that, while barely in her teens, her mother used her as "bait" to attract boyfriends, who would give the mother money for drugs. At this early age, Valerie was introduced to sex and drugs, particularly crack before she was fourteen. Her mother lost all parental rights for abuse and neglect. Valerie learned early how to use her charms to get men to do what she wanted. It was fortunate that her foster-mother, whom she called her stepmother, had encouraged her to finish high school and enroll in a tech-school computer course. Valerie was a good worker, when she worked, but for years she moved in and out of the drug scene. Ky hoped that she would get help this time, but knew that he could no longer help her.

He again tried to get Valerie to release him from representing her in these cases. "You won't cooperate with me," Ky told her. "You fail to appear in court, and you don't listen to what I tell you. I've gone as far as I can with you. This has to be the end of the line."

"Mr. Gearan, I promise you I'll cooperate this time. If you don't take my cases and get me outta here, I'll call Verna."

Verna! That's it. Valerie holds a trump card -a hole card - and is willing to play it. What other choice is there?

"Okay, I represent you, but first I need to talk to the arresting officers, the narcotics agents, before asking for a bond hearing. Will you help them out by making a few buys for them?"

"Yeah, yeah - I'll help, just get me outta here."

Ky talked to Officer Lee and Sergeant Wilson of the drug squad. They didn't want to put Valerie back on the street until she had time to dry out and detox.

Valerie threw a tantrum when Ky told her she needed a couple of weeks to dry out. "Get me outta here. Now. If you don't, I'll call Verna."

He calmed her down by promising her a bond hearing within two weeks and told her he would leave some money at the front desk so that she could buy sodas and candy. He left the jail, feeling that no good could come of any of this.

The bond hearing was held a few days later before Judge Moore, a colleague and friend of Gwyn's.

Ky rose from his courtroom chair. "Your Honor, may we approach the bench?"

"Permission granted."

At side bar, the assistant district attorney and Ky outlined to the judge the plan agreed to by the narcotics officers.

"The defendant is released upon her promise to appear," the judge ordered, and continued the case until two o'clock on Monday, February 1st.

Valerie leaped to her feet and followed Ky into the hall. She rewarded him with a cozy hug.

"Thanks for your help, Ky. I knew that I could depend on you to get me out."

"Remember to call me next week, Valerie. We need to discuss your case. Be sure to see Officer Wilson and Sergeant Lee on Friday."

"Oh, I will," Valerie said, hugging Ky once more. "I will."

She left the courthouse with her stepmother. Somehow, Ky still felt anxious about Valerie.

By the end of the following week, Ky had yet to hear from Valerie, and called her stepmother. "Have you seen or heard anything from Valerie?"

"Not since Monday, Mr. Gearan. She said she was moving back in with Howard. He doesn't have a telephone. Do you want me to call Howard's mother and leave a message for them to call you?"

"That's not necessary," Ky said. "I'll probably hear from her in a few days."

Ky secretly hoped that he had seen the last of Valerie. The week before the hearing, he called Sergeant Lee. "Has Valerie contacted you?"

"Not since the week after the bond hearing. She was supposed to have made a buy for us last night but was a no-show. Guess she got cold feet and has absconded."

"Thanks for the information. If she calls, I'll have her contact you. Her trial is set for Monday."

On Monday, Ky walked into the third-floor courtroom. A few defendants and lawyers were there. Judge Moore was presiding. Ky did not see Valerie in the halls or in the courtroom. The clerk called her case. Ky stepped up to move for a continuance when Judge Moore spoke.

"Mr. Gearan, approach the bench, please."

Ky approached Judge Moore, who requested that he meet with her during the break. Ky wondered again, Where is Valerie? Why haven't I heard from her? What does Judge Moore want to see me about?

Soon he had his answers.

Ky entered Judge Moore's office, and she greeted him with a worried look on her face.

"Please close the door. Mr. Gearan, a client has made a serious accusation against you. I talked to Valerie in the hall this morning. She told me that you were pressuring her to have sex, and that she had gone to the screener to have Mark Grant appointed in you stead."

"Judge, this is all untrue. All this is untrue."

"I believe you, Ky. I must follow the guidelines and refer this matter to the local grievance committee. The worst news is that the new court reporter overheard most of her story. Gwyn will be heartbroken. Finally, the Chief Judge has requested that you not handle any indigent cases while this matter is being investigated."

"Judge, I'll take myself off the list. There are only two or three cases that have been set for trial."

"When are these cases set?"

"Near the end of the month, Judge."

"Very well, you have permission to handle these pending cases. I will notify the Chief Judge. I'm so sorry. I'm so sorry."

With head held down, Ky left Judge Moore's office. He moved slowly through the hall toward the elevator. He saw no one, as his head was bowed, knowing that his days as a trial lawyer would soon be over. Most of all, he dreaded what he would have to say to Gwyn.

Then Ky began to think about the new court reporter for the *Daily*. He was introduced to Sean Tighman one day in late December while on the elevator. Blaine, the outgoing reporter, had introduced him, but Ky barely acknowledged Sean, being preoccupied thinking about his trial in Superior Court that afternoon. Funny, how he could remember details - Sean's dirty blond hair, acned face, rumpled trousers, tobacco breath, nicotine-stained fingers, and scuffed shoes worn down at the heels.

Would it be payback time now for his lack of common courtesy? This story would be a coup for Sean - a scandal with lots of juice: the sexual escapades of a lawyer whose wife was a judge. Sex and politics.

Ky wasted no time when he returned to his office. He drafted a letter to all current clients: *Effective April 1st, I am closing my law practice. You may pick up your files at the office during business hours, 9-5, Monday through Friday.*

He had his secretary send out statements to clients, and he paid all outstanding bills. Then, he had to face the task of telling Gwyn. He had to tell her before the courthouse rumor mill cranked up and shifted into high gear.

Chapter Three

Ky had gone to a meeting of the Juvenile Justice board after work that day. He arrived home around seven and picked at his dinner. He watched TV but couldn't concentrate because of the dread he felt at what he had to tell Gwyn.

That evening, after 11 o'clock, Ky was in the bathroom at their home, brushing his teeth, preparing for bed. Gwyn was reading a novel by Scott Turow, wearing a pink flannel, granny gown. Ky was wearing his blue shorty pajamas, which he wore both winter and summer. Ky approached the bed. "Gwyn, I've got to tell you. I don't know how, but I've gotta tell you."

"Tell me what, Ky?" She put down the book and took off her reading glasses.

"The Chief Judge has removed me from the indigent counsel list."

"Oh, is that all?"

"No, there have been accusations, accusations and charges against me."

"What accusations, what charges, who brought them?"

"They were brought by Valerie, a drug client. I represented her on similar charges over two years ago. She told Judge Moore that she wanted new counsel, as I'd been pressuring her for sex, and wouldn't represent her unless she gave in. This is not true. The judge has sent these charges to the local grievance committee. They, no doubt, will interview her, and I fear that she will tell them of sex we had two years ago."

Gwyn's face turned crimson. Her jaw was set. She was furious, but was trying to control her anger.

"Tell me, Ky, are you having sex with her now?"

"No. It was just the one time over two years ago."

"How could you? How could you? Why did you do this to me - to us - to our marriage? To our children? What if my mother and your mother find out? Be glad that your father is dead. This would have killed him."

. Ky began to shake like he had the chills. Feeling a bit faint, he sat down at the foot of the bed. He sobbed and buried his face in his hands. "I'm afraid everyone will find out. The *Daily* reporter was in the hall when Valerie told her story to Judge Moore."

"Ky, why would she tell such a story? This will hurt my re-election chances. The *Daily* always endorses my opponent in the judge's race. You know that."

"Gwyn, I think I know what happened. Valerie was supposed to make a drug buy and got cold feet before she was to go into a crack house that the narcs had been watching. She panicked, and thinking that she would go to jail, she cooked up this story to get another lawyer appointed and at least buy herself some time. Perhaps, she thought that this story would get her off. While in jail, she kept mentioning Verna to me and used her as a threat. She said she'd call Verna if I didn't represent her on the drug charges. I told her I wouldn't, until Verna was mentioned."

Gwyn got out of bed and stood facing Ky. "You mean you let this crack whore blackmail you, don't you?"

Ky hung down his head, he couldn't face her. "'Fraid so, Gwyn. I was scared that she would bring up the sex we had two years before. I've allowed myself to be a victim, but the greater victim is you and my family."

Ky raised his head and looked at Gwyn. "Why did you think Verna might be involved in setting you up," Gwyn asked.

"Guess she's still angry about those damn dresses - the letter I sent to her demanding payment and threatening suit. It's a real good way for her to get even with all of us - you, Fiona, and me. I felt a lot of repressed hostility and resentments in her. Expect she's gloating now."

"Tell me the truth, Ky, have there been others?"

Ky got up from the bed and turned toward her. "Yes, I'm ashamed to admit - these affairs began soon after you moved out of the office suite and became a judge. No excuse of any kind can I offer. Yes, some were clients and former clients."

Ky started toward the door. Gwyn sobbed. "How could you...? How could you? Oh, our poor children. Oh, my God....our marriage won't survive this...Oh, Ky. Tell me one thing. Have you stopped these affairs?"

"Yes, too late, I'm afraid. But, yes, I have. I'll spend the night in Jason's room and will move out in the morning."

"Ky, stay in Jason's room for a while. Mother's moving into our bedroom at the end of the month, when she gets out of rehab for her stroke. Your not being here would raise questions that we don't need to answer now. I can take Fiona's room."

Ky went out the door and turned toward Gwyn. She was weeping again. "How could you? How could you? Ky, how could you do this to us?"

Ky knew now what a price he had paid, and would pay, for a few stolen moments. Still shaking, Ky climbed the stairs to Jason's room. He held onto the rail to keep from falling. He didn't turn on the lights, not wanting to wake Laurie Lea and Mitch. Ky hoped they had not heard what went on downstairs. He knew they'd find out soon. He prayed, kneeling by the bed. "Dear Lord, forgive me...forgive me." He could hear Gwyn sobbing downstairs. "Forgive me the pain I've caused my family...forgive me...and for the pain I will cause...forgive me."

A sleepless night. This was the end of things. End of the intimacy of nearly thirty years. Ky and Gwyn had met a couple of months after his discharge from the Army. A fraternity brother from Buchanan University had called him and asked him to meet him at Berwick during the Labor Day weekend. He had been dating Gwyn's roommate at the nursing school there. Ky was to meet Gwyn for a dinner date. He had been accepted to law school at Poteat University.

Gwyn had been a delight. Petite, light brown hair, big brown eyes, and a golden tan. She was bubbly and full of life, with a great sense of humor. He took an instant liking to her. At the urging of his fraternity brother, Ky drank a few beers before dinner. Soon, Ky had their corner of the Bridle and Stirrup Club rocking with laughter. He was telling stories and jokes that he had heard in the Army and in his salesman job that summer, and he was ad libbing jokes. His frat brother told him, "If your law career doesn't pan out, you can get a club job as a standup comic."

"Yeah, can probably use some of these stories in the courtroom. I understand the jurors like to be entertained."

Gwyn and her roommate were offended by some of the jokes, but Ky continued on. At the end of the evening, he was smashed and, the next day, recalled little about his drive back to the Dual Cities.

A couple of weeks later, Ky returned to Berwick and to Gwyn's dorm. He called for her at the desk and soon she came down, dressed in her starched uniform. "Ky, I've got to work a shift at the hospital, but you can give me a ride there."

"Okay. I wanted to apologize to you for my gross behavior at dinner the other night."

"Your apology is accepted. I knew that you had too much to drink.. That can happen to any of us, at times."

"Could I propose a 'make up' dinner date, say Saturday night?"

"Yes. I would like that. I have no classes or duty at the hospital that day."

She got out of his car at the hospital entrance. "Shall I pick you up at eight?" Ky asked.

"That's fine, Ky, looking forward to it." She turned at the door and waved to him. He waved back and drove off.

On Saturday, they went to the Leipzig in Kilmont for dinner. The evening was enjoyable for both of them. By year's end, they had become engaged, and married the next summer, soon after Gwyn's graduation. They moved into an old house on South Center Street in Waiteville, a few blocks from the law school and lived in an apartment upstairs. Every night at midnight, the "Palmland Special" roared down the tracks at the rear of the house. The house would shake and wake up Gwyn and Ky.

Three other married students - divinity, premed and military science majors - also lived there with their wives. By spring, all the wives were pregnant. Ky found it well nigh impossible to shave in the morning, as both bathrooms were occupied with sufferers from morning sickness.

Jason was born the day the spring semester ended. Ky was so proud the day Gwyn and their son came home from the hospital. After Gwyn returned to work at the hospital, Ky took care of Jason. When school started, Gwyn worked the night shift, so Ky could be with Jason. They bonded as a family. Ky's delight knew no bounds.

Ky had been with Gwyn for all these years, except for a brief separation after his termination as house counsel for the trucking company about ten years ago. He had been seething with rage, anger and resentment over the way he had been treated by the new owners, a multinational that had bought the company. Though he refrained from drinking, Ky soon discovered an outlet for this anger - a sexual attraction to younger women.

During his first year back in private practice, he had lunch with a client who had brought a friend along. The friend was a slender, brown-haired divorcee who had the carriage of the dancer she had been.

The next Saturday, the woman called him at home. Gwyn and Laurie Lea were working in the yard.

"Ky, this is Paloma. We had lunch last week. You mentioned that your daughter had a horse for sale, as she was going overseas. Is it still for sale?"

"No, she has shipped it off to my younger daughter's school in Maryland."

"Sorry to hear that, Ky. I had promised my two daughters a horse for Christmas. I did enjoy lunching with you."

"How about lunch one day next week?"

"Good. I work out Mondays at Silver's Gym. We could meet at noon in the snack bar."

"Thanks," Ky said. "I'll be there."

Ky arrived a little early and watched Paloma's aerobics class. They had lunch in the snack bar, which overlooked the indoor pool, and then drove to the top of the Sentinel, a mountain ten or twelve miles from town. They got out of the car and walked to the parapet. It was foggy and soon they returned to the car. Ky opened the door for Paloma, and he moved to kiss her at the door. She pulled away and then turned toward him and said. "No, Ky. I'm so vulnerable now. I've just broken up with my boyfriend." Ky kissed her, and she returned his kiss. They began a brief, mostly nonsexual affair, as she had a young son at home.

At that time, Gwyn was occupying a suite at the end of the hall in Ky's office building. It didn't take long for her to become suspicious about his long lunches and late arrivals in the mornings. Gwyn had overheard a telephone conversation and learned about the affair. When Ky returned from a trial that afternoon, he got a call from Gwyn at home. "Your clothes are in your car." She hung up. Ky tried to call her back, but she had taken the phone off the hook.

He went down to the car. Yes, most of his clothes were there. How did Gwyn find out? Is this it for our marriage? What am I to do now? Ky called his minister. "Sorry to hear what has happened," he said. "Stay in touch. Let me know the phone number and address of where you'll be staying. Let's hope that it is only temporary. I'll talk to Gwyn if she calls me."

Gwyn didn't call the minister. That was her way. She kept in everything. Ky believed that Gwyn's early years - the time she spent in an orphanage, where she had been placed by her mother - had taken their toll. She had learned to cope - learned too well. She had never forgiven her mother for placing her there, when she took that job at the Battenberg County farm. She was the live-in nurse, on call twenty-four hours a day.

Ky found a room-by-the week at the Blue Bird Motel off I-44 on the Glaston Highway. It was a good location, only ten minutes from the office. Ky was at the office each day at six. Gwyn continued to come into her suite at nine each day. He arranged to be at the courthouse at that time. They did not see or talk to each other that first week.

Paloma, the divorcee, came by only one night that week - baby-sitter problems. The sex was unsatisfactory. Ky had already made an unconscious decision to end the affair.

Gwyn had changed all the locks at their home. Mitch had installed a chain lock on her bedroom door. At the end of the week, Ky went by to talk to Gwyn. She was in the den reading book. He knocked and entered. "Gwyn, please let me come home."

"Is the affair over, Ky?"

"Yes, it's over. She pressured me to go to Las Vegas for a divorce. I told her I didn't want that. When I told her I was still in love with you, she became furious and called me everything but a child of God. She left the table at the café where we were lunching, cussing all the way out the door. Yes, it's over. It's over."

Gwyn surprised Ky with her answer. She put down the book she was reading and took off her glasses. "You can come home Ky on two conditions. First, you must agree to go to marital counseling with me and, most important, agree that you will never have another affair."

Ky sat down in relief at the news. "Yes, Gwyn, I will. Yes, I will. I've been miserable for the past week. Now I know what our marriage and our home has really meant to me."

"Okay, Ky, go ahead and check out of the motel. You may move your things back in this afternoon. We start counseling Monday."

Now, years later, Ky again had confessed his infidelity to Gwyn. Once she learned of the affair with Valerie, they became strangers living under the same roof. Soon, they maintained an uneasy truce and were especially polite to each other. Ky always knocked before entering Gwyn's room, which was usually locked.

One Monday morning in April, he knocked on her door, bearing orange juice and tea. "May I enter, Gwyn?"

"Come on in, it's not locked."

Ky entered her room. She was wearing a blue quilted robe, bunny-fur slippers, and eyeglasses. She put down the newspaper. Gwyn always read everything in the paper before going to work, while Ky barely scanned the headlines. He had thought that the local newspaper had gone down hill since the Gordon family sold it to a Virginia conglomerate. At one time, the paper received state and national recognition for its reporting and features; now, it seemed to Ky, the paper existed for selling advertising copy for the suburban malls.

"Gwyn, I'm trying my last case this morning. It was postponed from last month, as you were juvenile judge then."

"How do you feel, Ky?"

"Usual butterflies. I had them before my first case nearly thirty years ago and now for the last one. Always thought that the day I didn't feel butterflies, I should retire. So, I'm not ready to quit the practice, but know I must. Call it damage control. My not being at the courthouse every day may help your re-election chances. Guess that's the least I can do for you now."

"That may help some, Ky. However, if the *Daily* publishes articles about you, it will make little difference as long as you are in town.

Ky knew that being a judge was the most important thing in her life. For a long time, she wanted to practice medicine. Her mother was not able to send her to medical school, and Gwyn went to nursing school instead. She had turned down a Fulbright Scholarship to marry him. She would have made a great diagnostician. He recalled her diagnosis of Laurie Lea while she was being treated in a small hospital in Germany. The symptoms indicated typhoid, a diagnosis that was confirmed when Laurie Lea returned to the States. Gwyn had used these skills in the courtroom; she had a knack for penetrating to the heart of a case and rendering a good decision.

"Gwyn, out of an abundance of caution, I've retained Frank Folder to represent me in these matters. Hope there won't be any stories in the *Daily*, but I feel there will be. A likely result of these stories is that they will spawn lawsuits for malpractice. Also complaints may be filed with the state board."

Gwyn put down the newspaper and her face brightened as Ky told her of retaining Frank. She turned towards him and said, "That's good news; Frank can help you if anyone can. That makes me feel better knowing he is helping you."

Ky had known Frank since law school. His specialty was defense work, both civil and criminal. He would be an asset in the defense of any claims. Ky put on a light topcoat, and walked slowly down the steps to the garage. His shoulders slumped and his head was lowered. He knew that soon, he would no longer live here. "Damn...damn...damn," he muttered under his breath as he backed the car out of the garage.

He handled his last case in his usual workmanlike manner. The juvenile had broken into a school band room and had stolen a trumpet. The judge gave him a year's probation, fifty hours of community service, and an eight o'clock curfew on school nights. Ky hoped the boy would use this chance to straighten out, as his next offense, or if he violated his probation, would mean a year in training school. He had always handled these cases, even though they paid little, as this was the only chance for many of these young offenders to live a useful life.

Ky left his office after lunch and walked the three blocks to the Old Courthouse, at Freedom and High Streets. Across High was Frank's office. He had done a good job of restoring a 1920's department store building. Other lawyers soon followed and the block was no longer blighted. Ky entered the reception area. It had been decorated with reproduction Queen Anne-style furniture. The carpet was a Persian original. Frank always had good taste, Ky thought.

Ky was ushered into Frank's office by his secretary. She was a tall blonde and was dressed in a gray suit. "Mr. Gearan, may I bring you a cup of coffee?"

"Please, with just a little cream."

Frank's office was plush - an Oriental carpet lay on the walnut parquet floor, walnut paneled walls, green leather sofa and matching chairs. Frank had a massive walnut desk with a matching sideboard. Aviation and yachting magazines were on the walnut coffee table. On the walls were pictures of Frank's Lear jet and his oceangoing sailing yacht. There were pictures of Frank's two children and an oil portrait of his second wife. Frank had gone into the law profession to do good; he had done quite well.

"Here is your coffee, Mr. Gearan."

Frank came in wearing a black cashmere blazer and dark gray slacks. His blue shirt was set off by a tie in the gold stripes on black of Poteat University. "Sorry I was a bit late," he said. "I was lunching with the board of visitors of the law school.

"That's okay, Frank. This morning I tried my last case. I'm retired as of today."

"Why did you retire, Ky? Thought you were doing very well in your practice."

"Thought it may improve Gwyn's chances for re-election. Particularly since I face bad media exposure."

"You needn't worry about Gwyn. All the trial lawyers of both parties are supporting her. She should have little trouble defeating that former assistant DA. She isn't even popular with her own party people. How did you feel trying your last case?"

"Frank, I felt about the same. Trials are trials. They're more alike than different. I think it was you who asked me the difference between district court practice, and Federal court practice, and transportation law cases when I first returned to the practice. I told you there was little difference. I recalled saying, 'Today I represented a man who stole five hundred dollars from his employer. Three months ago, I cross-examined a president who had looted five million from the stockholders of his company. Same people.' Guess we all have larceny in our hearts."

"I don't know what I'd do if I couldn't practice law. My whole life is wrapped up in being a lawyer," Frank said.

"I'll do all right. I've never tried to confuse my identity with what I do for a living. I do have a M.B.A. from Poteat. May do some management consulting. You recall I had other duties at the trucking company. They included marketing and executive management. There're lots of things I can do, but I probably couldn't do them here in the Dual Cities."

Frank excused himself to make a telephone call. "Sorry about that. I had to talk to a lawyer down in Williams County about a proposed settlement."

"What's the next step? Where do we go from here?"

"Not anything, now. Until the newspaper publishes or suits are filed, we wait. The local grievance committee will report in a month or two. Most likely they will send your case on to the state grievance committee, as you are too hot a potato to handle locally. Your greatest danger is malpractice suits. If and when the newspaper publishes, then suits are sure to follow. You may remember the Commissioner Hyde case in Williams County. When the allegations of bid rigging appeared in the papers, a rash of suits were filed. Most had no merit, but we had to settle some."

Ky shuddered. He had heard the sentence of doom.

"We have to fight the battle on two fronts - in the courtroom and at the state grievance committee. I have assigned Dugald White to handle the court cases, and Saul Friedbourg to handle any grievances."

Ky felt relieved. He knew both attorneys. Dugald was a top student at Poteat Law. He married a local girl and began practice with a classmate. He then joined Frank and had been in the firm nearly ten years. Dugald was a mid-Westerner, a son and grandson of lawyers, plainspoken and direct, and thorough in preparing his cases. "Meticulous" came to mind. Ky was pleased.

Saul had been born in the Bronx, but moved as a child to Ardmont in the mountains of the state. His father had bought a small woolen mill there. One day, Ky was talking to Saul about a client who had survived the death camp at Mathausen during World War II. The client couldn't let go his hatred of the Nazis. Then Saul told Ky that the members of his family who had remained in Poland had perished in the camps. This, he said, was the impetus in becoming a lawyer - helping those in danger of losing their life and liberty. He had been a great defense lawyer. None of his clients had suffered capital punishment.

Ky appeared as a witness in Federal court for one of Saul's clients accused of malfeasance in public office. The previous administration had brought many minority public officials to trial for various offenses all over the country. Saul's client was one of three acquitted in Federal court in Glaston. Saul's keen intellect, soft-spoken manner, and consummate courtesy made him effective with witnesses, jurors, and judges.

Before Dugald and Saul came into the office, Frank summed up Ky's plight. "Perhaps one of your greatest failings has been the inability to say, 'No,' to a client. The cases that you don't take are not the ones that hurt you. I think this failing will be costly not only in money, but also your law license."

Dugald and Saul entered the office. Dugald outlined his research. His contact at the newspaper's law firm indicated that no decision had been made on publication. Saul reported that the local grievance committee would send the grievance on to the state. Frank cautioned Ky not to talk about his case and to refer all questions to his lawyers.

"Ky, you've been in the Army: 'name: rank and serial number.' That's the drill: 'No comment.' 'Check with my lawyers.' We are at war. We can expect no favors."

"Frank, I've moved most of my furnishings out of the office. I should get the rest of them today. You know my home number. I'm supposed to go on a continuing legal education trip to London and Paris in June. I'll furnish telephone numbers and hotel names later."

"Ky, we'll do what we can to cut your threatened losses and mitigate the damages."

"Thanks, Frank, I'll try to stay I touch."

Ky felt a little better as he walked down Freedom Street on his last trip to his office.

Chapter Four

Ky left Frank's office and stepped out into the bright April afternoon. He walked down Freedom Street to his office. At Salt Street, a block from the office, he noticed a Volvo had stopped for the light. The driver was Paloma. She saw him and turned her head away. Had it been ten years? Ky looked straight ahead. He could see the Brethren Bonnet "Pod" (cover) in the Czech of the Brethren on the front of his building. His affair with Paloma had lost its cover, and now his other affairs would lose their cover. The *Daily* would blow everything out into the open.

When he entered his office, Ky began to remove and pack the few remaining items. He had already sold his books, bookshelves, secretary's desk, filing cabinets, and copier. He had given his computer and printer to Laurie Lea, and moved the furniture in his private office over the weekend.

He took his diplomas and professional licenses from the walls. Ky took down the Daumiers, a gift from Gwyn, and two watercolors of Oriente Island painted by Fiona. The Daumiers he would give to Gwyn for her judge's office, and the watercolors to Fiona to hang in her new home in Glaston.

Then he took down the picture of Gwyn and the children. Finally, he removed the group photograph of the international law class in London, taken some fifteen years before. He picked it up. How young they looked! How happy they were - no work - no children - just classes, tours and time together. That summer was Ky's first in Scotland. He felt at home there from the first day of the trip.

Ky and Gwyn had renewed their marriage on this trip. A year later, Gwyn graduated from law school. In another ten she was elected judge, and now.... those affairs. Why did he start them? Why did he tell himself that they wouldn't harm his marriage? Why did he lie to himself? Why did he deny his addictive behavior? Regret began to seep in like a slow toxin.

31

Looking at the boxes that summed up his life as a lawyer, father, and husband, Ky felt that they were all that was left of thirty years of family and professional life. Thirty years that he could not live over. Only regret remained. It had moved in to stay.

Ky picked up the box of diplomas and licenses and moved to the door. Merry Lee, the lawyer next door, burst in. "Ky, there's a reporter on the phone asking questions about Sarah, who used to work for you. Please talk to him."

He went next door and picked up the telephone. "Ky Gearan, here. You were asking about Sarah?"

"Yes, Mr. Gearan. I'm Sean Tighman, a reporter for the *Daily*. I'm trying to find Sarah. Do you have her telephone number?"

"Yes, she's still at the Deaconsgate condos and has a listed phone."

"Thanks, Mr. Gearan. I need to see you, too. I'm coming up to your office now."

"What do you mean, 'need to see me'? My office is closed!"

"Don't get upset, Mr. Gearan. I just want to ask a few questions about some of your clients."

"Questions about clients? Can't answer questions about clients. This information is confidential."

"Some of them have already talked to me, Mr. Gearan. Who can I ask questions about your relationship with them?"

"No one," Ky responded. "Any questions should be referred to my lawyers."

"Who are they, Mr. Gearan?"

"Folder, White and Friedbourg." Ky hung up knowing that his cover was being blown. He called Dugald and told him what had happened.

"Be cool, Ky. You did the right thing. He won't call us, I'm sure. We know how to handle him."

Ky loaded the boxes into his car and returned to his home. Regret accompanied him. That afternoon, Sarah called him.

"Mr. Gearan, this reporter came by my condo and asked questions about you."

"What was his name?"

"He said it was Sean Tighman and that he worked for the *Daily*. He asked me if I knew you had had sex with clients. Stuff like that. I told him that you had always been a perfect gentleman around me and around your clients. He kept on and on. I finally told him, 'Honey, half the lawyers in this town are having sex with their clients, and the other half with their secretaries.' He didn't seem to like this answer and left in a huff. Reckon he'll print that?"

"Doubt it, Sarah. Really doubt it. Thanks for calling. Let me know if he contacts you again."

"I will," she said. "What was he up to?"

"Don't know, but definitely he was up to no good."

Ky wondered how he had found out that Sarah had worked for him. He decided to call Virginia, a former secretary. "Virginia? Ky Gearan, here. How are Jeff and the kids?"

"They're okay, but sometimes I think I need to go back to work to rest up. Not enough hours in the day for all I have to do. Heard you're closing the office. What'll you do?"

"Right now, not much of anything. I plan to go on a continuing legal education tour of London in June. We also go to Paris. Beyond that, I don't know. Perhaps, I will use the M.B.A. to do some consulting. Did a *Daily* reporter contact you/"?

"Yes, but I didn't say anything. Oh, I said I had worked for you nearly five years and left to stay home with my children. He then asked questions about specific clients, but I didn't recognize any of the names. They must have become clients after I left. I did tell him I couldn't answer questions about clients, and that I didn't appreciate such questions. He hung up abruptly."

"Thanks, Virginia. If he calls again, let me know. Give my best to Jeff and the kids."

After Ky hung up the phone, he thought of the employees who had worked for him over the past ten years. There was

Virginia and Sarah; Rochelle, a very loyal secretary; and Paula, who had moved to Georgia. He felt good about them. They wouldn't do him any harm. He was grateful that he had treated them well. Other lawyers said he had spoiled them. Ky knew that secretaries and paralegals could make or break a lawyer, particularly a sole practitioner. Being kind and considerate paid off.

He was disturbed that Sean had found employees and had talked to clients. He wondered how Sean had found out who they were. Then he thought about clients with whom he had affairs. Ky hoped they wouldn't give him trouble, but he couldn't be sure - couldn't be sure at all. Had the reporter already interviewed some of them? He tried to squelch his fears about the clients that he had made passes at; this was a source of anxiety. The ache returned to the pit of his stomach.

The next day, Ky received a telephone call from Hilda, a former client. "Mr. Gearan, this is Hilda. A reporter's been over here asking me and Amber questions about you. What the hell is going on?

"What did he ask you, Hilda?"

"He wanted to know if I thought you were a pervert? I told him that I was gay and that I thought all men were perverts. He then talked to Amber for a few minutes."

"What did Amber tell him?"

"I don't know. She left for work right afterwards."

"Tell me, was his name Sean Tighman?"

"Yeah, he showed me an I.D., a press pass or something, with his picture. What was he trying to find out?"

"Hilda, I don't know, but he's no friend of mine. Call me if he contacts you again. I'll give you my home number, as the office phone number won't answer after the end of the month."

"I will. Amber still wants you to come by the Golden Lobo and see her dance. She says she owes you a lap dance."

Ky hung up. Amber was a slender blonde with green eyes and fair skin - the type of woman he must stay away from now. He had helped her out in a couple of cases, and she had been grateful. That's all behind him bow. No more cases - no more affairs.

He wondered again how Sean had found out about Hilda and Amber. These were appointed cases, and records of indigent cases were available at the Office of the Courts. These records probably could be accessed by computers at the courthouse. It had to be a lawyer, one of the clerks, or an employee at the Office of the Courts. Some of this information would be covered by the State Privacy Act, but payment records were public.

Near the end of the month, he received a telephone call at home from a Mrs. Bryan. She was the mother of a minor that Ky had represented in a mental commitment case three or four years earlier. She was irate.

"Mr. Gearan, I'm Mrs. Bryan, Deborah's mother. This reporter came into my apartment and began asking me questions about you. He didn't show an I.D. or anything. I'm mad at myself for letting him in. He then wanted to talk to my daughter alone. I told him 'no way,' and I told him I didn't know you, and to get out of my house. I'm still mad. I'm calling the paper to complain."

"Mrs. Bryan, had your daughter been a patient at Oak Hollow Hospital?"

"Yes, when she was fourteen. I signed papers at the courthouse to have her sent there. I didn't know what else to do. She had been climbing out the window at night, meeting her boyfriend, smoking dope, and having sex. I'm a single parent, a night nurse, and couldn't watch her all the time. She was released before going to court. I never knew she had a lawyer."

"I do remember the case. I interviewed your daughter along with other minors in the dayroom. The case was dismissed when I went to court because she had been released. That's why you never met me."

"Mr. Gearan, for a time I felt guilty about sending her to Oak Hollow, but it scared her into behaving. She gets top grades in school, dropped the scumbag boyfriend, stopped the drugs, and plans to enter State this fall. She wants to be a teacher."

"Glad to hear that. Thanks for calling, and if he contacts you again, please call. I'll give you my home telephone number."

Ky became more anxious after her call. Mental commitments and juvenile cases are in locked files. They are not public records, and juvenile records are sealed. They cannot be used against them when they become adults. It has to be someone in the Clerk's office or in the Office of the Courts.

Who in the Clerk's office would want to harm him? Could it be that the Clerk was still angry over Ky's support of another candidate in the primary two years earlier? Ky had been incensed at the Clerk for removing the executor and manager of his client's father's estate. The action resulted in the failure of the family business, the estate's main asset, after a petition was filed by the client's sister - the estranged wife of the executor. After the hearing, Ky and his client got on the elevator. "There ain't no justice...there ain't no justice," the client complained." A lawyer, overhearing his lament, replied, "If you want justice, go to a whorehouse; if you want to get screwed, go to the courthouse."

Ky didn't join in the laughter. He was seething when he entered the bailiff's lounge. He told the defense lawyers what had happened in the Clerk's hearing, the removal, and the award of five thousand dollars from the estate to the lawyer who got the removal. They laughed, and one of them said, "Where have you been? That's just home cooking in the Clerk's 'kitchen.' Don't you know who the favorite cooks are?"

Ky mentions the name of the lawyer.

"That's the chief cook. Hire him and get the result you are looking for."

After he returned to his office, Ky called the woman who was running against the Clerk. He told her he would support her campaign and mailed in a hundred-dollar contribution. The Clerk won the primary easily. It's not the Clerk, Ky told himself; no one could hold a grudge and be that small - not for a hundred-dollar contribution, surely. Has every indigent case that I've handled been under scrutiny? What can I do about this?

How many cases? Several hundred in the last five years? Ky pounded the desk in the den. He felt powerless and helpless.

Who would sue him over these cases? He remembered the halcyon days when lawyers sued doctors and not each other. He knew that there were lawyers in the state who specialized in suing other lawyers. What happened to honor among thieves?

Ky picked up the *Daily* and put it down. He had met the editor, Eldora Johns, some ten years before, when he ran for the State House. He recalled going into her office. He saw her A.B. from Smith and her M.A. in journalism from Columbia, and many pictures of her getting awards or shaking hands with prominent politicians. On her desk was a picture of her father shaking hands with a former president.

"Ms. Johns, I'm Ky Gearan, a candidate for the State House."

She stubbed out a cigarette in an ashtray, and said, "Tell me, Mr. Gearan, why are you running for the State House? Have you ever been elected to public office?"

"No, Ms. Johns, I've never been elected, but I'm interested in education. I want to see students get a college education, tuition-free, at state schools, if they've maintained a B average in high school and maintain that average in college. If Louisiana can do this, why not our state?"

"Seriously, Mr. Gearan, you don't think the legislature would adopt such a bill? Our taxpayers are burdened enough as it is."

Ky felt that there was not much sympathy for his candidacy here, and excused himself. He ignored a copy of her book, which had just been published, on the corner of her desk. Hindsight now told him, he should have bought a copy and had her sign it. All he knew was that the *Daily* had endorsed his opponent in that race and in three other races. All of his campaigns were unsuccessful. Gwyn had never been endorsed by the paper in her two races, either.

He felt sure that the *Daily* would support the former assistant District Attorney, the darling of the police force, over Gwyn.

Her nickname among cops was "Tough Tessie." He knew that being a judge had become the most important thing in Gwyn's life. Now he was fouling up the chances for her re-election. Ky knew that he was carrying too much baggage and would have to leave town, maybe leave the state, or even the country. He would have to go into exile, if she were to have a chance in her race. Leaving the practice had been only a partial price he would have to pay. There was no way to prevent the *Daily* from printing stories about him or mentioning that he was the husband of a District Court judge.

Regret hung like a carcass around his neck.

Chapter Five

"Any messages for Ky Gearan?"

"Yes, Mr. Gearan." The attractive blonde receptionist handed him a message. Ky had returned to the Dorchester Hotel after the tour group had visited the Tower of London. This was the dreaded, but expected, message.

He looked at the message: *Call Laurie Lea Gearan immediately.*

It was a little after four in London; she would be at home on a Sunday morning. Ky went to his room and dialed her number. She answered on the second ring.

"Dad, it has hit the fan! The lead story complete with your picture - the Sunday edition. You are now a social pariah. You can't come home again. Do you want me to fax the article to you at the Dorchester?"

"No, I don't want the hotel employees to know about this." Ky thought how silly that sounded. After all, the Sunday *Daily* went to a dozen counties with a circulation of a hundred and twenty-five thousand.

"Laurie Lea, how many of these alleged affairs are reported?"

"At least eight or ten, I stopped reading at that point."

"And your mother?"

"She didn't want to read any of these accounts and doesn't want to talk to you. I took it upon myself to call. She has locked herself in her room and has turned the bell off her phone."

"Another reason for not reading the article, is that down the road I'll be cross-examined about it. I don't want my memory clouded by someone else's account."

Ky recalled his conversation with Laurie Lea and what she had told him when he returned home after work on Friday:

"Dad, the reporter, Sean Tighman, came by the house around four o'clock and demanded to see you. He kept asking and hanging against the door. I told him that you were not there, and

I didn't know when you'd come home. I ordered him off the property, and when he balked, I chased him out into the street. He got in his car and left. What do you think he wanted?"

"Laurie Lea, he is going to publish. Reporters always ask the person being written about to confirm or deny what will be printed. This is newspaper standard operating procedure. This story will be out in a day or two. Nothing we can do to stop it."

"Dad, are you going on that London and Paris trip tomorrow?"

"No reason not to, and every reason to go now. Was your mother here when he came by?"

"No, she just came home a few minutes ago and is in her room. Do you want me to tell her you're here?"

"No, don't bother her. We'll eat Mexican tonight if you want to."

They went to dinner at seven. Very little talk about anything at the table. When he returned, Ky packed his bag and laid out his clothes for the next day. At ten, he turned in, as he never slept on planes.

Ky slept only an hour or two; he couldn't sleep. He got up, unpacked and repacked his bag, discarding certain items of clothing and adding others. He tried to read a book about Britain called *Sarum*. Bert, the tour director, had suggested they read it. He soon gave up and turned on the late, late movie. The next day, he remembered little of what he had seen. Up at five, Ky went on his morning walk. He was careful not to wake up Gwyn's mother, who had moved into their bedroom a couple of months earlier.

At eight, he took orange juice, toast, and tea up to Gwyn's room. He knocked and was invited in. She was in bed reading the paper, and had also been awake most of the night. They talked about everything but the pending publication.

"Gwyn, I don't want to go on this trip without you. I had forgotten, when I signed you up in January, about the required judge's conference the last week in June."

"Guess, it's just as well I'm not going, Ky, since everything has happened and will happen. Besides, I'll have to take mother along, as she can't stay by herself."

"Reckon you're right, Gwyn. I would have loved to revisit those places that meant so much to us on our previous trips."

"Ky, I told mother I would take her to that wedding in Campbellton. We'll leave here around twelve. Let's don't say anything in front of mother - anything that might upset her."

Gwyn came into the den where Ky was waiting around twelve-fifteen. "Ky, sorry we are a few minutes late leaving. Took a little longer than I figured to get us ready."

"It's all right. The trip to the Capital City Airport is only a couple of hours. I'll have plenty of time before the flight leaves."

Ky was riding in the back seat of the sedan because Gwyn's mother needed to recline; her medication made her drowsy. Ky wanted to talk to Gwyn, but couldn't risk upsetting her mother. He thought about what he would say, if he could talk to her.

"Gwyn, I do love you, even though at times I've had a poor way to show it by my behavior. I know saying 'sorry' won't get it with you. 'Sorry' is not good enough. some how, some day, some way, I'll make amends to you for the hurt and harm I've done to you. I'll begin by moving out of town when I return from the trip. I plan on taking that master's course at University College-Glaston. I'll move there or farther away if you want me to. Staying in Europe is another possibility. The Isle of Skye would be a good place. There, I'd be among friends and clansmen. I know I cannot now ask your forgiveness, as I've got lots of amends to make first. Perhaps, the best amend would be to live a different life from what I had been living. I can tell you that I do love you and that I regret what has happened, and maybe someday, I can ask your forgiveness."

Ky did not expect Gwyn to say anything to him at this time. The hurt was so deep, that she had retreated far into herself. That was her way, when hurt and threatened. On the surface, she could appear cool and calm, and could do her usual good work.

He felt that she had been shattered beyond repair, and that he had done it. He had broken Gwyn's life and now must pay.

"Gwyn, this is the airport exit. Hope I haven't made you late for the wedding."

"We've got plenty of time."

They pulled up to the curb at the International Departure Terminal. Gwyn said, "Have a good trip, Ky."

He looked at Gwyn with tears streaming down his face. He hugged her and kissed her, thinking it would be their last. She clung to him tightly and wept. He slowly got out of the car. She was still weeping. He stood at the curb until the car disappeared from sight, and then he walked into the terminal.

Ky went up to the airline counter. "Here's my ticket to London, and my passport. I'm checking one bag. I'll carry on the shoulder bag."

"Very good, sir. Boarding begins at seven, at Gate 6. Have a good flight."

Gwyn's voice echoed, "Have a good trip."

Gotta hold it together, Ky told himself, "Gotta. It's only a week."

"Ky, you're the last one here. Come on into the lounge and meet the others." It was Bert, the tour director, a lawyer from Capital City. He was tall and heavyset, with brown curly hair, balding on top. Ky followed Bert to the lounge. At the door, he paused, and spoke softly to Bert.

"I need to tell you something in confidence. I think there will be an unfavorable story about me in the newspaper in the Dual Cities. Don't think that we need to tell the others."

"Sorry to hear that, Ky. I'll be silent."

Bert introduced Ky to the group. He knew Theo, a law school classmate, and met Cora, his wife; Bob, his roommate, an assistant attorney general; and two other couples from the eastern part of the state.

Theo's blond hair was graying at the temples, and he had put on some weight, but his six-foot frame carried it well. Cora's hair was brown, with some blonde highlights. She was tall and had green eyes and a fair complexion. His roommate was of medium height, wore thick glasses, and was nearly bald. A wispy gray hair was combed over to cover one of the bald spots.

The lounge was all chrome and glass, with blue vinyl upholstered chairs. A waiter came up to the table and asked Ky for his order.

"Soda water, with a twist of lime, on the rocks."

Theo exclaimed, "Ky, what a change! You used to like your beer a whole lot."

"You're right, I did. Haven't had a drink now in more than twenty years. Gwyn was going to throw me out if I didn't stop. Besides, I couldn't handle it - never could. Guess I was a slow learner."

The group all laughed at Ky's words.

"Don't guess I need to offer you a cigarette?" Theo asked.

"No. I stopped smoking a few months after I quit drinking. It was harder to stop smoking than drinking."

"Gee, Ky, you have no bad habits now?"

"Can't say that, Theo, still got plenty of them."

They had spent an hour or two in the lounge, talking and getting acquainted, and they ate a small snack that was served to them in the lounge. At six, Bert announced, "Time to go through the security. Takes longer now, since all those bombing scares."

Ky tried to sleep on the crossing, then tried to read a Patricia Cornwell mystery, but soon gave it up. He finally dozed a few minutes before the plane landed at Heathrow. There, a minibus met the group and drove them to the Dorchester Hotel.

"See you all in thirty minutes here in the lobby," Bert said.

Ky went up to this room. He quickly shaved and changed shirts and socks. He met the group in the lobby, where they soon departed for the Tower of London. It was a three-block walk. Ky was grateful for the exercise; it seemed to restore him.

After the telephone call to Laurie Lea, Ky felt a strange peace. Somehow, he knew that the *Daily* could not define him. He knew who he was - had always known. He took a short nap before meeting the group for dinner.

Before dinner that night, he talked to Bert and told him about the bad publicity. "Bert, on Wednesday morning, I may go to Euston Station and take a train to Scotland, to the Kyle of Lochalsh and the Isle of Skye. If I'm to catch the train, I will have to leave the hotel at six. If at eight, I'm not in the lobby, go on to the channel port without me. So don't wait, I'll be gone."

After dinner at the Cheshire Cheese, Samuel Johnson's pub on Fleet Street, Ky returned to his room alone. His roommate was going to a club in SoHo. He began to relive the events of the past. He reminded himself that he had to stay in the day - stay in the moment. Ky got his notes together for the presentation the next day at Gray's Inn. He had been invited to be on a joint panel of English barristers and American trial lawyers. Ky reviewed the program, and looked at his picture and brief biographical sketch:

> *Gearan, Kylmor: Lawyer, b. Allister Co., NC, 1941; A.B. Buchanan U., 1962; J.D. Poteat U., 1967; M.B.A. Poteat U., 1982; U.S. Army, 1962-64; m. Gwyn Davy, 1966; four children: Jason, Mitchell, Laurie Lea and Fiona: Member, ABA; Fellow, American Trial Lawyers.*

The program at Gray's Inn, one of the Four Inns of Court, was to be a mock criminal trial. It was the opening session of the continuing legal education program. Ky was able to concentrate his mind in preparation for his presentation. Had he not been living his life in compartments? He was a trial lawyer, flawed husband, neglectful father, pursuer of beauty, and failed political candidate. Didn't all of these describe him?

He arrived at Gray's Inn a little before the others. Ky walked into the Great Hall, looked at the massive table made from the oak timbers from Sir Francis Drake's "Golden Hind." He could see through the arched window, the ancient, bent, and gnarled Catalpa tree planted by Sir Walter Raleigh. He had brought the sapling back from the New World. It had survived nearly four centuries and the Nazi blitz of 1940. This tree would survive into the next millennium. Ky felt that he probably wouldn't. He remembered again that summer in London fifteen years ago, when he and Gwyn had taken international law. One lecturer was Edwin Edwards, Q.C., a Welshman. He was a barrister, Queen's counsel, and a Liberal Party member of Parliament. He took Gwyn and Ky, along with other law students, to visit the inn. They noticed a statue of the Griffin of Wales in the center of Holborn Street outside. He explained that this inn had been founded by Welshmen, and had been favored by them since the 14th century.

Ky thought back to the American Bar Meeting in London some ten years before. Gwyn and he had attended a garden party and reception, hosted by Gray's Inn, for the members of the American Bar Association. Ky felt like an unofficial member of the inn who was returning home - a fellow barrister.

Today, Ky was to appear in the mock criminal trial. Fellows of the inn, English law students, and U.S. lawyers were there. The trial was to be tried first under American law and then English. The facts were simple: a botched hold-up of a small shop and the shopkeeper was killed. A closed-circuit video camera recorded the events. Ky was chosen to prosecute the U.S. case. The video was admissible under U.S. law, and the jury of English law students convicted the defendant. Such evidence was inadmissible under English law and the defendant was acquitted. Ky was congratulated for his victory. His face reddened with embarrassment; it was an open and shut case. After the trials, Ky made a short presentation on U.S. criminal trial practice and then fielded questions. Here, he was in his element, quick to think on his feet, with the instincts of a boxer. When he finished, he felt the satisfaction of old - for a job well done. He knew that this was what had motivated him, not outward success or the fruits of victory, but the inner satisfaction of a craftsman. Public approval had meant nothing to him. Approval? Laurie Lea's words echoed: "Dad, you are a social pariah…" He knew he would soon find out how inner-directed he really was. The test would surely come soon, and he was powerless over the outcome.

At noon, lunch was served in the Great Hall. Ky lifted his water glass in toasts to the Queen, the master of the inn, and to the senior fellows of the inn, and then sat down. He was joined at the table by his friend Edwin Edwards. Ky was preoccupied and barely kept up his end of the conversation. After dessert, he excused himself and returned to the hotel.

At breakfast the next day, Bert asked where he had gone. "Did you forget the tour of Lincoln's Inn?"

"No, I had to return to the Dorchester and make a phone call to my daughter, but she was out. I used the afternoon to take a nap. Still behind on the sleep I lost on the flight."

"Are you going to the Old Bailey with us this morning?"

"Yes, and to the Houses of Parliament this afternoon. Perhaps, we'll see Edwin Edwards there. He is one of the few Liberal Party members left."

The Old Bailey - the criminal courts - housed both trial and appellate courts. No court was like it in the States. He remembered the criminal appeal that he and Gwyn went to as guests of Edwards that first summer in London. He marveled at how the judge, at the end of the arguments, dictated his decision and order directly into the record, referring to few notes, citing most of the cases from memory. "It's not as easy as it looks," Edwards had explained. "These judges serve long apprenticeships, defending and prosecuting cases, at least twenty years, for most of them. It's similar to a concert pianist playing an hour, without sheet music, apparently effortlessly and flawlessly, to the audience's amazement. What we don't see is thirty years of daily practice."

Ky and the tour group entered the Old Bailey around nine that morning. Security was tight. Uniformed and plain-clothed policemen ringed the street outside and were posted in the halls. They cleared a security gate on the ground floor and again on the third floor. IRA terrorists were being tried across the hall from their case. Their case was tame by comparison - securities fraud

- white-collar crime. The defendants stood in the dock, a railed-in partition, in the well of the courtroom. All wore dark suits, white shirts, and somber ties. The judge and barristers were robed and wigged.

Ky's thoughts began to wander: His mind was back in the States, reading a newspaper story, Laurie Lea's words ringing in his ears. The group left the courtroom at twelve for luncheon recess. Ky sighed with relief. They went to a pub frequented by barristers. Ky tried to eat fish and chips, washed down with ginger beer, but he had little appetite.

The group left the pub at two, and walked down the Thames embankment to the Houses of Parliament. It had been sunny and warm all week. They joined a tour that was just beginning. At four, the group left the Houses of Parliament. Ky went back to the Dorchester, while the others went on a pub-crawl.

Ky called Laurie Lea; she was at home. "Bad news, dad. Your story went out yesterday by the Associated Press to all the newspapers in the state. This is big news, dad, and it's not going to go away. Dad?...Dad? Are your still there?"

"I am speechless. What else can happen? Oh, now I remember why I called you. Laurie Lea, can you get me in that therapy program that you went to last year in North Dakota? Think it was ten days, and was called 'Total Immersement' - or something like that."

"No, dad, you have to already be in therapy to attend, but tell me, how did you know?"

"Know what?"

"That mom, Fiona and I are trying to find a place to send you. Are you amenable?"

"Yes, I am. I need to go somewhere."

He had been given the gift of desperation - the willingness to become willing to seek help. This was the First Step. Laurie Lea and Ky had always had great rapport. Each could sense what was going on with the other. Ky very well knew that she was angry at what he done, and he dreaded the consequences of it.

Before dinner that night, Ky talked to Bert. "Remember, I may catch that train, 'The Flying Scot,' in the morning. Don't wait if I'm not at the bus at eight."

"Okay, Ky. If I don't see you, have a good trip."

After dinner, he packed his bag and called the front desk for a six o'clock cab in the morning. He recalled happier days on the Isle of Skye. He knew his friend, Rob Don, curator of the island museum, could find him a crofter's cottage to lease near the Clan Donald lands. Gilda and Harold at the Island Inn would let him stay there, until he found a place of his own, should it come to that. He salivated thinking of Harold's salmon and trout. The inn was the only place in the world where he would be served four or five potato dishes at the same meal. The dishes were all different and all delicious. Best of all, no telephone, no TV, no newspapers, and no civil process servers. Gwyn could sell some of his stock and send him a letter of credit to the Bank of Alba. He had English pounds and credit cards. With these comforting thoughts, Ky soon fell soundly to sleep, a night without dreaming.

He awoke at five, shaved, showered and dressed, and turned on the TV in his hotel room. The news was on. The newsreader told of a job action, a strike of the workers on the national railroads. This was the third Wednesday in a row that the trainmen had halted work. The union was flexing its muscle. Ky knew it was too late to get a flight to Glasgow, and commuter connections beyond were uncertain at this time of year, with fog and turbulent winds.

Ky went down to breakfast at seven. Bert greeted him warmly, grasping his hand. He was eating the full English breakfast. "Glad to see you, Ky. You look rested. Ready for our trip to Paris?"

"Yes, I'm looking forward to it."

The bus was on time. They boarded at eight and in about an hour were at Dover. They took the hovercraft to Calais and boarded a bus to Paris. They were in the outskirts of the city in a little over three hours. Somehow, Ky thought it was meant to be that he go to Paris, and accepted it. He looked at many familiar landmarks. Ky dreaded visiting them; they would bring painful memories of the happy days with Gwyn. Without her it wouldn't be the same again - never again would it be the same. It didn't have to be that way. Regrets.

On Thursday, after a short visit to Notre Dame, the group went to the Palais Justice. There, the halls were filled with French trial lawyers - *avocats* - dressed in gowns and hats, just like those in the Daumier prints that had been a gift from Gwyn; now they hung on the walls of her office at the courthouse. They met an *avocat* who spoke flawless English. He agreed to take them to a trial. It was an action for divorce. He noted that one of the three judges was a woman, and wished Gwyn could witness the trial.

Bert whispered," Where is the juror box and the jurors?"

The *avocat* replied, "There is no jury in a French trial. The judges hear the evidence and apply the law to the facts as they find them." Gwyn does that every day, Ky thought. There is no jury in her court, but parties have the right to appeal in criminal cases and receive a trial by jury in Superior Court.

The divorce was contested. The parties were hostile. Ky could tell that there was real hatred between them. Counsel were courteous with each other, but the parties looked grim. Ky was determined not to act this way with Gwyn when they settled their marital property. He would be more than fair. He felt that she deserved it all - just-compensation for his treatment of her. She had earned every penny. She was due a bonus for all the grief he had caused her.

The group lunched at a small bistro. Later they walked to the Tomb of Napoleon. Ky became depressed at the sight and wondered how many had been killed in all the Napoleonic wars. Guess this is where we all end up - the end of all our striving - for the arrogant and the meek. Except the meek inherit a plot 6' x 6' x 2' - while their oppressors sometimes inherit a marble tomb.

They bought baguettes, fruit, and cheese on the walk back to the hotel. Ky walked with Cora, Theo's wife. Somehow she knew of his distress, which had penetrated his cheerful façade. She appeared to be a friendly, generous, and compassionate person who genuinely cared for people. "What's troubling you, Ky? Can I help?"

"I've got my troubles. You've helped already by your concern. Thank you for your kindness."

He wished he could fast-forward his life and move beyond his present pain. Ky knew that was not possible and he would have to move through it all - that was the only way.

Back in his room that night, Ky again thought of flight. He knew that there was a boat-train that left the Gare D'Orsay that went to Victoria Station in London. Perhaps, he could board it tomorrow night and continue on his way to Scotland? He kept his counsel and said nothing to Bert. He would see what tomorrow would bring.

After a breakfast of croissants, juice, and tea, he left on the early-morning tour to Versailles. He saw little while he was there, even though he looked at everything. He was in the flight mode. The group had lunch and went back to Paris and to the Louvre. He saw again the armless Venus, and wondered why he had worshipped for so long at her shrine. Ky knew that he had a fatal weakness for beauty, and felt that now was payback time for his years of slavish devotion. Ky moved on to the Mona Lisa and marveled at the enigmatic half-smile. On the surface, beauty - the rose - and beneath it, the thorn. Did her lover harvest both rose and thorn? The tour group moved on to the next gallery. Ky lingered in front of the painting. Cora came back and squeezed his hand. "Thanks," Ky said.

They left the Louvre and went to the Eiffel Tower. All went up the elevator, except Ky and Bert.

"Ky, I've always had a fear of heights, and it has become worse the older I get."

"I understand. I've always feel a bit queasy when I go to high places. Don't have that feeling at all in planes. Somehow, it's different."

Ky had no real desire to jump, but he didn't want to test it in his present emotional state. He had such feelings only once before, while a freshman in college, when an unrequited love affair was ended by the girl. At that time, he sometimes thought of jumping over the rail and down the stairwell and ending it all. He got over it after a few months, and had no such thoughts since.

The group came down from the tower. Two of the couples left together, leaving Ky, Bert, Cora, and Theo, who suggested they share a cab. Ky replied, "No, let's catch the Metro. It's already five, the traffic will be bad now."

They took the Metro, which was crowded. They had to stand. Theo moved to the door at a stop. Ky shouted, "Theo, not here! It's the next stop, Place Clichy."

Ky got up to leave at the next stop and was barred by three Algerians with outstretched arms. He pushed the middle one out to the platform, where he landed on his butt. Another one went into his fanny-pack and took his wallet. Ky got off, felt that his wallet was missing and started to get back on, but quickly thought better of it.

Theo asked, "How much did they get?"

"They got it all - everything but my passport and a few coins." Ky's thoughts of flight evaporated. Without cash and credit cards, he would have to return to the States. Flight was not meant to be.

When they returned to the hotel, the airline agent gave each of them a cash refund of thirty-five dollars for an overpayment. Ky used the refund to dine and used the change to tip the maid. He slept soundly on his last night in Paris. With resignation had come peace.

At seven, the bus left for Charles DeGaulle airport. It crept through the early morning traffic, and soon they were moving through the suburbs. Urban sprawl had come to Paris. Ky looked at the ugly blocks of concrete flats - not the Paris tourists' dream of.

They were herded down long passageways and through security. Once cleared, they boarded the flight to the States. Ky no longer wondered who might meet him at the Capital City Airport, or what might face him when he returned to the Dual Cities.

Chapter Six

"Mr. Gearan, meet your party at the Economy Car Rental counter in the outer lobby."

Ky had just cleared customs at the airport. Moving into the outer lobby, he looked to his left toward the car rental counters. About halfway down, he saw a tall bald man with a red beard. Ky recognized him at once, a reporter, really a photojournalist, who covered political events throughout the state. Still wearing that sagging khaki safari jacket and carrying the press camera. No friend of mine; not here to pick me up and take me back to the Dual Cities. Ky quickly turned to his right and out the door to the driveway. Next to the curb was a newspaper rack. The *Trio Weekly* was displayed in the window of the rack. The lead story, complete with picture, read: "Dual Cities Lawyer's Harem at Public Expense, page 5."

Ky had now returned to the real world. He was grateful that he had seen the bastard first. He spotted his brother-in-law, Bryan, across the driveway, parked next to the traffic island. Bryan offered to help Ky load his bags in the silver station wagon, but Ky declined, as he had only the two bags.

Bryan was retired military, still wore a crew cut, and always a coat and tie. He was neat to a fault. His troops in the First Marine Division had ironically nicknamed him "Pig Pen," for wearing starched and pressed fatigues in the front lines.

Ky's sister, Cheryl, had married Bryan a year after he had graduated from Annapolis. He served in the South Pacific as an enlisted man during World War II. He was posted to Korea and saw combat there a few months after their marriage.

Bryan was in many ways the opposite of Ky, conservative in the manner of life and in politics. He lived in a gated country-club community near the ninth fairway. Cheryl used the proceeds from the sale of a family-owned business to open a string of computer stores, which she and Bryan jointly managed. After a few years they sold the business. With some of the proceeds, they bought a beach house at High Dunes, near Port Canmore, on the Outer Banks of the state. Ky and Gwyn had been guests there.

Bryan paid for parking at the gate and they headed west on I-44 to the Dual Cities. It was a bright day, and Bryan put on his sunglasses. "How was the flight?"

"Uneventful. The weather was clear all the way from Labrador and Newfoundland to the Outer Banks. We must have flown over your beach house, as the plane turned to the west at Port Canmore.

"How was London and Paris?"

"London was great. Returned to Gray's Inn again, the Old Bailey, the Houses of Parliament, and the Tower. Paris was, well, different. Saw the usual sights, but my pocket was picked on the Paris Metro. Laurie Lea told me not to wear that fanny-pack. I didn't listen and lost all my cash and credit cards. Fortunately, I was able to call and report the theft. Don't think I'll suffer any loss. It will be a hassle to replace them. I didn't lose my passport, but I'll have to get another driver's license."

Bryan didn't mention anything about the newspaper articles, for which Ky was thankful. Ky dozed a bit in the car. At Glaston they were delayed because of road construction, and when Bryan stopped, Ky awoke. In the Dual Cities, Bryan exited onto Avon Road. Evidently, they were not going to Ky's home.

"Your mother wanted you to spend the night with her."

Now all his fears were realized. That was the last kiss at the airport. Had it been only one week?

They soon turned into the long drive into the Bowmar Estate. Ky's denial of the last few years began to peel away. The denial that those casual relationships didn't matter to his marriage, to his family and to his profession. Denial had informed him that he could survive the fallout from the Valerie affair, but the *Daily* had blown his cover. Nothing now could save him.

Emma, his mother's maid, met him at the door of her condo. "Ky, I don't care," she said. "I love you." She gave him a big hug. He smelled the pleasant cooking scents on her clothing. Emma was a light honey color, with deep laugh lines etched in her pleasant face.

His mother was in her wheelchair behind Emma. "My son, my son, my only son. I love you, I love you." She was still red-haired, in her mid-eighties, still freckled with blue eyes, still the Irish lass. She would say that she was Scotch Irish and not Irish. Her mascara had run, as she had been crying.

Ky was grateful for their warm greeting, but felt that he didn't deserve it - that he was not worthy of their love. It was a moment of grace, and he almost let it slip by. He realized that he had to make many amends to those that he had hurt, and would have to start with his family. He thought about grace and knew that the nature of grace was that it was unmerited and undeserved. Sometimes, grace happens.

His mother had bought her condo from the former CEO of the Richards Tobacco Company. It was built of stone in the French Chateau style to harmonize with the great house on the Bowmar estate. His mother had redecorated, replacing everything but the tile floors and parquet floors.

Ky took his bags to the upstairs bedroom. Through his window, he could see the roof of Bowmar House. He unpacked only a few a soiled items from his bag, as he was leaving for an unnamed treatment center on the morrow. He washed out the few items and hung them on the shower curtain rod to dry. He lay across the bed and dozed. Jet lag had caught up with him.

Ky woke up and looked at his watch it read: "6:10, July 2, Saturday." So yesterday was July 1, the day his pocket was picked. At least he had called the credit-card companies to notify of them of the theft - one less thing to worry about. He washed his face and went downstairs.

"Ky, I've got fresh green beans, potato salad, sliced ripe tomatoes and coleslaw," Emma said. "The cornbread is ready to come out of the oven."

"Emma, that sounds great. English food and French cooking can't come close to your cooking, and you've got iced tea with sprigs of mint."

Ky ate his fill and had seconds on the green beans. Emma opened the refrigerator and exclaimed, "Surprise in the refrigerator - banana pudding."

"That's the way I like, Emma, cold and soggy - I mean moist." Emma filled his glass with more iced tea, and said, "Glad you didn't lose your appetite."

"That meal was superb. My compliments to the chef."

Emma went to a table near the bay window. "Oh, I almost forgot, this letter came for you. Gwyn brought it over."

It was from Seth Layton, his partner in the office building. Ky read it with grateful heart. Seth had understood what had happened. This understanding was forged during the twelve years of their partnership. They had gained respect and concern for one another. Ky's spirits were lifted. "Lift up your hearts..."

He wondered why Gwyn and the children hadn't come by or called. He knew it was more than just awkward for them. He hadn't heard from his friends and under the circumstances, he didn't expect them to call. He couldn't imagine what he would say to them were the circumstances reversed. Later, Laurie Lea did call to tell him they would be over at ten in the morning. Now he felt much better.

"Ky, do you want to see Sunday's paper and the other articles about you?" Emma asked.

"No thanks. I don't plan to read any of them."

Ky knew that he must not read any of the articles. He must keep the avenues of memory open. This memory must be his and not that of others. Perhaps he was not yet ready and willing to look at the consequences of his behavior. The irony did not escape him. It was a paradox: He was overexposed by the media, but at the same time isolated and hidden from public view. Maybe he was still in denial - that the person described in the media was the *real* Ky Gearan - but he knew that the person depicted there was the one the public would judge. He had already lost in the court of public opinion; he was now awaiting sentencing. His true freedom had already been lost.

Around ten, he withdrew a pair of pajamas from his bag and went to bed. The nap had taken the edge off his sleep. He slept fitfully and arose at five. Ky went for his morning walk around the bounds of the Bowmar Estate. He went by the canebrake, the bamboo grove. There was a whirr of wings, a flash of red and black. Red-winged blackbirds! Were these the same birds that nested at Oriente Island? This was the place where he and Gwyn had had a cottage. He could see his boys at play among the dunes; Laurie Lea dog-paddling in the shallows; and Fiona asleep in the hammock under the cottage. He and Gwyn enjoying each other in the long lazy afternoons. Elysian Fields were his! Were those the happiest of days? The birds disappeared from sight.

He walked on around the estate and saw the great house, built in the Thirties in the style of a Loire Valley chateaux. Sadly, the owners never lived in the house. The husband died and was buried at sea. His widow stayed in the stables, as she had received death threats from workmen who had been paid a pittance for their labor. At her death, she willed the house to Poteat University. Years ago, he and Gwyn had attended a party at the Bowmar stables when Gwyn was in law school, at a student's apartment there. Some of the land had been leased to a builder who built condos there. Ky's mother had moved in her condo shortly after his father's death.

At eight, Ky joined his mother for a breakfast of tea, toast, and oatmeal. A little after ten, Gwyn, Laurie Lea, and his son Mitch, came to the condo. Laurie Lea was tanned and healthy; she worked out and ran every day. Gwyn looked drawn and was subdued in manner. She had frosted her brown hair since he had seen her last. She was wearing a simple yellow sundress with matching sandals. She was not wearing her wedding ring.

"Ky, how was your trip to London and Paris?" she asked.

"It was okay. Except I got my pocket picked on the Metro. I should have listened to Laurie Lea."

"Yeah," said Laurie Lea. "You sure should have."

Emma said, "Miz Gearan's not feeling good this morning. She sends her excuses."

"I'll go keep her company, Emma," said Laurie Lea.

"Thanks, she'll appreciate the company," Emma said.

With her long straight brown hair, high cheekbones, dark eyes and slender build, Laurie Lea looked like her Cherokee ancestors. With her appearance and her knowledge of Arabic, Hebrew and Farsi, she could travel freely throughout the Middle East.

At eleven, Jason and Fiona arrived. Jason was a younger, more slender version of Ky. Mitch, with his honey blond hair and brown eyes, was tall and resembled Gwyn. Fiona was a little taller than her mother, but had her features. They came up and hugged Ky. He burst into tears again and couldn't say anything.

A little later, Jemmy McRae, his minister, arrived. She was a large graying woman in her fifties and was divorced with grown children. Ky wondered what she was doing there, but returned her hug at the door. He became concerned when Bill Huston, a chaplain from Poteat University, showed up. He shook Ky's hand. He wore a crew cut and had a neatly trimmed beard. He was also a professional clown who entertained children in the hospital. Why was he here?

When Joan Westbrook, Fiona's therapist appeared, Ky knew it was an intervention. He had been on an intervention team for the state board in February. Dr. Westbrook was a tall, slender bookish-looking blonde with thick horn-rimmed classes. "A group of your family and friends have gathered here this morning," she said. "We are the intervention team. We are here to help, not to judge or punish you. I'll be the facilitator."

So, he was now the intervenee - quite a switch in roles in a few months. Gwyn led off the intervention with a list of grievances committed by Ky over the years, both to her and to himself. Ky was sitting on a low stool in the middle of the group. Tears of sadness and anger began to flow.

Jason spoke and broke down and wept. "Dad, how could you - how could you?"

Ky began sobbing uncontrollably. Laurie Lea and Fiona told similar stories as Jason's, about how Ky's behavior had affected them.

Mitch followed. "I understand, dad. I'm like you in many ways. I understand."

Grace happens. Tears of happiness mingled with those of anger and sadness. Ky broke down completely when Jason shared that a friend in Atlanta had called him after reading the article.

Ky could never forget Fiona saying that unless he got help, he would be unable to visit with any of her children that she might have. The pain, the guilt, and shame overwhelmed him. He excused himself and went to the bathroom. He washed his face with cold water, but the marks of weeping remained. When he came back into the living room, Fiona said, "Ken's coming over at one, we're going with you to Los Angeles and to the treatment center. It's called Del Cara Hospital and specializes in treating multiple addictions."

"Thanks, Fiona, and thanks to you all. Please pardon all my weeping and loss of control. I do hurt."

At two, Ken, Fiona, and Ky left for the Glaston Airport. By three, they were winging their way to Del Cara and to an unknown future for Ky.

Chapter Seven

"We are approaching Los Angeles International Airport. Seat backs and seat trays should be in the upright position; fasten your seatbelts, please."

"Oh, dad, I forgot to ask you. Did you bring some socks? If you didn't, Ken will send you some."

"I think I did, Fiona. I'll check and see. If I didn't, I call you from the hospital."

Fiona was sitting in the seat in front of him. Ken had been airsick, even though it was a fairly smooth flight. He and Fiona had been married a little over a year. They had met at a Grateful Dead concert. Fiona had met her abusive first husband, Wallace, at a Grateful Dead concert, too. She had been living near San Francisco when she was married to Wallace. He couldn't forget that telephone call early one May morning two years ago. It was Fiona. She had escaped from Wallace, after he had held her in a scissors hold for five hours. Gwyn told her to go to a battered women's shelter and she and Ky would come and get her. Ky thought about that early morning flight to San Francisco and meeting her at the shelter. Soon after she returned, she met Ken, and they were married a year later.

Their plane landed on time. They didn't go to the baggage area, as Ky had only a carry-on bag. Ken and Fiona didn't need any luggage since they were returning on a flight that same evening.

"Dad, please excuse me, I need to go to the men's room."

"I'll go with Ken. Will you watch my bag?"

Ken was sick again. Afterwards, Ky wet some paper towels and washed Ken's face. "Thanks, dad, I think I'm better now. Should have known better than eat Chinese before boarding the flight."

They walked through the doors toward the cabstand, and got a cab. Fiona said, "Del Cara Hospital in Torrance."

"I know where that is," said the driver.

It was around midnight when they arrived at the hospital. They went through two sets of electronic doors, each locking behind them. A night nurse was on duty in his unit. "Good evening, Mr. Gearan, we've been expecting you. Sign this admission form. Did you bring the deposit?"

"Yes, I've got a check here. Tell me how to make it out and the amount."

Laurie Lea had given Fiona a blank check on her brokerage account. The deposit was half the amount for the twenty-eight-day stay.

Ky hugged Fiona and Ken. "Thanks ever so much for coming with me here. I've got the kindest kids in the world. Have a safe trip home." Fiona was crying when she left. Ky joined in with tears of his own.

Ky shuddered when heard the door lock behind them. He realized he was in a locked unit.

"Mr. Gearan, come with me to your room. It's the last one on the left."

The walls were painted a light blue, with a gray carpet in the halls. Ky looked into the room. No mistaking it for a luxury hotel. Three single beds and three metal wall lockers, and a small bathroom with shower. No frills. It reminded him of boot camp. Ky tried the mattress; it was hard. He complained to the nurse. "This mattress is stuffed with concrete blocks."

"Mr. Gearan, you can get a foam pad in the morning. Sleep well."

Ky didn't sleep much at all, as he was awakened each hour when the door to his room opened and a flashlight was shined in his face. So, this is suicide watch. Guess they watch all new patients. He had not thought of suicide and had chosen life regardless of the pain he was in.

Early next morning, Ky went to the nursing station to get his diabetes medication. He had turned in all his medications, and even his razor. He also asked for his razor so he could shave. He was no longer free and the realization hit him hard. At seven, Ky went in the cafeteria for breakfast. It was a small room with a few tables and a glass-fronted steam table where the food was displayed. He got a tray and got his breakfast. He looked around to find a table.

"Come on and join us." Three of the other patients were at a table near the window.

"Thanks, I'm Ky, the new kid on the block."

"I'm Mickey, this is Phil, and this is Robin, who just got off the bus from Jersey. He'll be your roommate. Phil has a ticket out of here today. He's going back to Memphis. We are seeing him off."

"Wish I were leaving, too." Ky thought again. Where would he go? Not back to the Dual Cities. Really he knew he had no other place to go. He had worn his welcome out at his own home, and couldn't go back there. Used up all his freedoms; had lost most everything. Had nothing else to lose.

Mickey asked, "We are wondering why you are here, Ky? Is it true that you haven't had a drink in over twenty years?"

Ky wondered how they had found out. He thought the intake form he'd filled out the night before was supposed to be confidential. "Yes, guess I was the 'dry drunk.' I was able not to take a drink, but everything else in my life became unmanageable."

Ky then said, "Guys, drinking is not my only addiction."

"Join the club, Ky," Mickey said.

"Ky, we have thirty minutes to walk if we are paired up and sign out at the desk," said Mickey.

"Robin, would you like to take a walk with me?" Ky asked.

"Yes. Three and one-half days on that bus have worn me out. Need to stretch my legs for sure."

Robin told Ky that he was a two-time loser. This was his second trip to a treatment center. The first one had been to a facility in Minnesota that was affiliated with Del Cara. He had relapsed by having sex with a former student who had dropped out of the high school where he taught. To avoid prosecution, he voluntarily entered treatment again. His teachers' union would pay for it.

They walked out of the hospital to an office park nearby, with landscaped grounds between the buildings. Everything was green; Ky noticed the irrigation outlets near every bush and tree.

"Ky, tell me about your alcoholism?"

"Reckon, I'm a classic dry alcoholic. Just like a wet drunk, except for intoxication and hangovers. Adrenalin was my substitute for alcohol. A good burst of excitement was like drinking two beers. I was an excitement junkie - trying cases, chasing women, running for political office - anything that created excitement. That's what brought me here. I broke boundaries with clients, and my story got in the newspapers. As a result, I lost my wife, family, profession, my reputation, and have been held up to public scorn."

"That's not fair, Ky."

"What's 'fair' got to do with it? What happened might not be fair, but it was 'just,' as in 'just desserts.' I'm not a victim. Can't forget that, I'm not a victim. Tell me your story, Robin."

"It began during my last year at a Calvinist seminary. I had secretly been dating the dean's daughter. She got pregnant, and had nothing else to do with me. I loved her and wanted to get married. The dean found out and kicked me out of the school. Hell, he didn't kick his daughter out of his family. I've got a fine son, now four. I visit with him on alternate weekends. Guess that will stop after this. I'll be found unfit. After breaking up with the dean's daughter, I became addicted to casual sex, and was hospitalized. This time, I tutored a seventeen-year-old dropout who was studying for her GED. She fell in love with me. We had sex. Her parents found out, and that's why I'm here. Eighteen is the age of consent in my state. Hope I don't lose visitation rights. My son means everything to me. You're a father, you understand."

"Yes, I do. Next to losing Gwyn, the love and esteem of my children is most important."

"Ky, there is an AA meeting at eight tonight, are you going?"

"Yes, if I have to. Why do we have to go to AA and other 12-Step meetings?"

"The program here in the unit is based on the 12 Steps; no frills, not anything fancy. It's like boot camp. No maid service; make your bed; clean your room. We get no time off except an hour or two every other Saturday to get a haircut, go to the drugstore, and to a coffee bar. Sometimes, on Sundays, we go on excursions to a park or to the beach. All strictly supervised."

At eight that evening, Mickey came to pick up Robin and Ky for the AA meeting. They entered the hospital meeting room. Chairs were placed in the center. At a table next to the wall sat an attractive blonde woman who was to chair the meeting. Twenty or thirty people from town had also gathered for the meeting. The patients sat in a group on the last two rows. The group was varied as to age, class, race, and gender. Ky felt a warm atmosphere, of closeness, of fellowship from the group. He began to feel a sense of belonging and felt less isolated.

The chair asked, "Is this anyone's first AA meeting? Give us your first name so that we may greet you."

Ky stood and said, "I'm Ky, and I'm an alcoholic."

He had said it publicly. Ky had made the first step to recovery. The meeting consisted of people who shared their stories - their experience, strength and hope. - with each other. Ky began to feel hopeful and a little more self-honest. That night he wrote in his journal: "You shall know the truth and the truth shall make you free." This day was July 4, 1994.

The next morning, Ky woke at five. His body was sore all over. He would ask for a foam pad for the mattress today. He felt as if he had been stretched on a rack. At six, he went to the nursing station to have his blood sugar checked, and his blood pressure taken. A small bronze man, with a warm smile, greeted him. "I'm Juan, the morning shift nurse this week. I will be taking your vitals signs this week."

"I'm Ky, came in on Sunday night. Glad to know you."

"I see from your chart, that you take medication for Type II diabetes."

"Yes, I do. Although I may not look like it, I am one-eighth Cherokee. We have a high rate of diabetes and alcoholism."

"Ky, this disease is also rampant in my family. I'm a Yaqui from Sonora."

"Yaqui? I've heard of your brave people and their persecution by Spaniards and the Mexicans."

"It is said that the Yaqui are at war with everyone. We had to stand alone. My people were enslaved and scattered."

"Juan, is that a Star of David that you are wearing?"

"It is. My people fled to a valley where there were Jewish people who had fled persecution in Eastern Europe. They were kind and gracious neighbors. The Church and the Mexican *Federales* had long treated my people like dogs - worse than dogs. We had no love for the Church or for the Federal government. Guess we shared a diaspora with them. It was not hard to convert."

Ky left with spirits uplifted. He had found a friend here. Juan had told him his blood pressure and blood sugar was in the danger zone. "Ky, you've been under stress. This raises your blood pressure, which raises your blood sugar. They move in tandem. Exercise is a good way to reduce stress."

Ky asked Juan to unlock the door to the patio, and he walked for thirty minutes. He meditated while walking. When he came back into the unit, he felt calmer.

A little before nine, Ky, Mickey, Robin and others met in a small room for group therapy. It was furnished with upholstered sofas and chairs. A beige carpet was on the floor. The walls were painted bubble-gum pink. The chairs and the two sofas had been arranged in a circle. Sharon O'Mara had been assigned to be their therapist. Mickey had met her before. "We're lucky," said Mickey, "she's the best - the toughest of them all. 'Tough love,' 'Get over it,' and 'Telling the truth and telling it faster,' are her slogans."

At nine, Ms. O'Mara appeared. She had red hair, fair freckled skin, was of medium height, slender build, and was wearing a green pants suit. Ky introduced himself and called her "Sharon."

"I'll call you 'Ky' and you can call me 'Ms. O'Mara.'"

After the group-therapy session, Ky entered Ms. O'Mara's office for his initial interview. He asked her if she were Irish. "Indeed. My mother was a Lynch, one of the twelve tribes of Galway. My father was an O'Mara. At fourteen, he stowed away on a ship at Cork, and jumped ship at Brooklyn. He became a plumber's helper and made a modest fortune as a plumbing contractor. His former partner served in the Nixon administration."

"Was he part of the Watergate conspiracy?"

"No, just a common criminal. He bribed some union officials. this was after he and my father had dissolved their partnership. I think some of the money did end up in the coffers of the Committee to Re-elect the President."

She handed him a copy of a disciplinary 'write up' report from his art therapist. "Patient appeared to be coming on to me in class, asking personal questions, and invading patient-therapist boundaries. His art does show talent, though minimalist in style. Uses no color."

"First day in class and you get written up. One more report and you are restricted to the unit, and another, you're history."

"Yes, m'am."

She looked at Ky's intake summary. "It says here that you're a trial lawyer, criminal defense attorney, effective in hanging juries. Also, it says you ran unsuccessfully for public office, but were effective in managing your wife's campaigns for judge. What were you trying to be, the poor man's Jack Kennedy?"

"Yeah, I reckon so."

"It looks like you've been looking for love in some wrong places."

"Aw, that's exaggerated."

"Ky, don't try to evade and minimize your behavior with me, and don't try to turn on that 'good ole boy' Southern charm.

It won't work. I have seen them all, and am on to you. Unfortunately, I married some of my mistakes: redneck; cad; cad; redneck..."

Ky liked Ms. O'Mara and felt he would enjoy working with her - even though she would tolerate none of his BS.

Mickey met Ky in the hallway after he left Ms. O'Mara's office. "Ky, I forgot to tell you that you need three affirmations for morning and evening meditations."

"Affirmations? Meditations? Thought this was a hospital. What is all this religious stuff?

"Ky, I found out that if recovery is to work at all, I have to seek the spiritual dimension of life. Detox can flush the booze and cocaine out of my body. Therapy can help reduce my craving, but the hole in my middle has to be filled. If it is not filled, then I relapse."

"Where will If find these affirmations?"

"Not to worry, they will find you. A clue is that they are the three things you need most in your life."

It took a few days of thinking and meditation, but Ky found his three affirmations.

"Be present." This was the first and hardest. He was always scripting the future and rewriting the past. He had one foot in the past and one in the future, and messed up the present. Ky was rarely in the moment.

"Let go of the outcomes." This was tough. He had always been goal-oriented. Results were what counted. Now the means became most important.

"Be compassionate to all living beings." Ky had tried to be kind to others. Now he must be kind to himself.

An unspoken affirmation informed all the others: "Cease clinging to that which changes." He had ignored this at his peril. His suffering resulted from trying to hold on to everything.

The defining affirmation: "I'm Ky, and I am sexually addicted."

The next morning, Mickey and Ky were finishing breakfast. "Mickey, let's go wake Robin and get him outta bed. We meet with Dr. Siegelmann at 8:30 in the dayroom."

Robin usually missed breakfast. He was severely depressed and slept a lot. The medication he took didn't seem to help. They woke him and he followed them into the dayroom.

"Good morning, men. I'm Dr. Siegelmann, psychiatrist in charge of the unit - the head shrink. Those of you needing a physical will get one after this meeting. While an AIDS test is not required, we recommend that you take one, and after the meeting a lab tech will take a blood sample."

All the patients signed up and submitted samples, except Ky. He told himself that he had always tried to be careful, but he really was afraid to get the test. Afraid of what he may find out.

On Friday, the other patients received the results of their test. All were negative. Mickey was elated. His frequent cocaine use had led to visits to massage parlors and pornographic bookstores, where he had engaged in anonymous sex and which had placed him at risk. Now he was relieved that he hadn't placed his ex-wife also in risk. After these results were made known, Ky thought more about the AIDS test. On Monday, he went to Dr. Siegelmann and arranged for a test. That afternoon, the lab tech took a blood sample.

The next morning, he asked the morning nurse, Bonita - nicknamed Rachet - when he would get the results of the test.

"In three or four days, just like the others did."

Thursday came, then Friday, and no results. Over the weekend, Ky began to worry. He scripted the worst-case scenario. Maybe it turned out positive and they are running a second test? Was I really all that careful? What about all those clients with AIDS that I visited in the jail? Had scrubbing my hands with antibacterial soap after these visits not been effective? What if? Why didn't I wear latex gloves like the jailers? What if?

On Friday of that week, he again asked Bonita about the test. "If you ask me one more time about that test…" Bonita warned.

Ky had really made her angry. At nine, he approached Dr. Siegelmann. "I'm worried I've no test results yet."

"Let me call the lab."

When he returned, he said, "Ky, they did send the test results over. They have been lost in transit or misfiled here in the unit. They're sending another copy over later today."

The next morning, Ky was summoned to Dr. Siegelmann's office. "The test was nonreactive."

"What?"

"It's negative."

Ky nearly collapsed with relief.

It was finally Saturday - the day for the outing to the drugstore, barber, and the coffee bar. Two hours. Strict buddy system. Pairs of two, and no wandering off alone.

The Japanese barber nearly shaved Ky's head. He wasn't going anywhere where anyone knew him, anyhow. Mickey was his buddy today. They talked and found that they both loved Irish and Scottish music, and shared those ancestral roots. Mickey was another two-time loser. Cocaine, massage parlors, and pornographic videos had destroyed his career as an investment banker. He had been making a six-figure salary. Worst of all, he was losing his wife and three children. Ky shared the same losses. He, too, had lost his profession, esteem of colleagues and was being held up to public scorn. Mickey was severely depressed but, like Ky, kept up a cheerful façade. He became the brother that Ky had never had and had always longed for.

Mickey had given him the best advice: "Always remember, Ky, if you put anything ahead of your recovery, that thing is the second thing that you will lose."

At the suggestion of Ms. O'Mara, Ky began to write letters to people that he had harmed. Those people he needed to make amends to. They were relatives, friends, colleagues, and clients. He spent Saturday after the outing and most of Sunday writing them. He found that the act of writing began to relieve some of his distress. Putting words on paper became a freeing experience. The power of the word. "A word fitly spoken" (or written). Why had he wasted so many words in his life?

Later Sunday afternoon, Mickey came to his room. "Ky, Father John is in the unit and he has agreed to serve us communion. The Bishop gave special permission."

Ky had met Father John the week before, and had asked him to serve communion. He never wore clerical clothing, instead wearing jeans and a plaid shirt. He was a recovering addict and alcoholic.

The patients joined in a circle in the dayroom. The priest said the comforting words and placed the wafers in their palms. Ky remembered the words: "Speak Thy word only and my soul shall be healed." He could feel healing slowly taking place in his life and was truly thankful.

Father John met with Ky after communion. He told Father John of his anxiety over the threatened lawsuits. "Do you have good lawyers," Father John asked. "Do you trust them to protect you and to defend your rights?"

"Yes."

"Do you have a Higher Power? Do you trust Him to protect you and defend you?"

"Yes."

The following week was Ky's turn to do his Fourth Step - a list of those whom he had harmed, and of those he felt had harmed him - at his group therapy sessions. He also made a list of his character defects and shortcomings. The list was so long it took two hours of group time. After he finished, he felt a burden lift from him. Ky was right in believing Ms. O'Mara when she said, "We are only as sick as our secrets."

At the next group therapy session, Ms. O'Mara passed around newspaper articles that Gwyn had mailed to her. Ky agreed to answer questions about his part in what was reported, but not anything that would break the rules of confidential client matters. At the session, Mickey looked at the first article and said, "Ky, this is a good picture of you."

Ms. O'Mara said, "Now, Mickey…"

Ky met with Ms. O'Mara privately and told her of things that had been on his conscience for a long time. She suggested he write letters of amends to those people, even if they were dead. Ms. O'Mara also suggested he do a Fifth Step on these matters. As instructed, Ky "admitted to God, to himself, and to another human being the exact nature of his wrongs." He chose Lawrence, a clinical psychologist who was also a patient in the unit, to hear his Fifth Step. After hearing his confession, Lawrence told him that he was not unique, and that he had also done some of the things described by Ky. Others had done them, too. Afterwards, Ky felt a sense of relief and of peace.

At five, on the third Sunday, Ky and the other patients met in the dayroom with Paul Irons, the Protestant chaplain assigned to the unit. Ky was poised between joy and dread. Joy at the fact Gwyn was coming, but dread as to what she'd say to him.

Chaplain Paul greeted them, "Good evening, men. We are going to do an exercise called 'The Man in the Pit.' Visualize you are a man in an open pit, the top of which is angled in so that you cannot climb out. Certain events will occur. Please record your reaction on the forms provided."

"The first event," Chaplain Paul continued. "A group of children gather and begin to throw rocks."

Ky wrote down, "Anger."

"The second event: A group of friends gather and peer down at the man and say, 'Oh, what a pity that he has fallen so low.'"

Again, Ky wrote, "Anger." The exercise proceeded, and to every event, save two, Ky responded, "Anger." He thought, "Have I been stuffing all this anger for all these years? Yes."

A face suddenly flashed before his eyes. "Ed!" He hadn't thought of him in years, not since the second grade at Ashland School. Every time he saw Ky, Ed would attack him, throw him to the ground and beat him with his fists. Ed never said a word. Ky also remembered a boy named Johnny, who would sporadically beat him on the school bus.

"Chaplain, is it possible that I've buried my anger about this all thee years?"

"Most likely. Anger is very destructive. It could have fueled your addictions. Sometimes I shudder when I think of all the repressed rage in our society. We pay a huge price for it. Look at road rage here in our state."

These words of the chaplain had lifted great weight from Ky.

Monday afternoon, Ky met Jason and Gwyn at the first joint session of Family Week. They had individual sessions in the morning. After the session, the families had a picnic served to them in the patio. Ky sat with Gwyn and Jason. He felt that this would be their last meal together.

At the end of the meal, Jason left the table.

"Gwyn, I'm prepared to tell you anything you want to know about me."

She asked very little, for which he was grateful. "Gwyn, I can't begin to make amends for all I've done to you. Guess the only thing to do is not to live the way I used to. That's the Ninth Step."

"Ky, I do love you, but I can no longer live with you."

"Gwyn, I've expected this. I can't risk inflicting harm on you anymore. I know my behavior has been killing you, physically, emotionally, and spiritually. Here is a letter I've written to you. Keep it and read it later."

She sat at the table a little longer, tears falling and silently sobbing, her chest heaving. Her face was red, and she put her head down on the table. Ky wanted to touch her, but he was afraid, after what he had told her and she had told him. He got up and went over to talk to Jason, who was seated on a bench in the corner of the patio.

"Jason, please begin to forgive me for the way I've treated you. I know I've harmed you beyond repair. The only amend I can make is not to live the way I used to. Forgive me."

Jason got up with tears in his eyes and silently hugged Ky.

At nine, Ky went up to his room alone. Gwyn and Jason had returned to their hotel. He was now alone, truly alone.

On the last day of Family Week, a Thursday, Ky met with Gwyn in a corner of the patio. "Gwyn, this is the last time I'll see you for a while. I plan to move to Glaston when I return. Maybe I'll move to the mountains. Hate to go into exile, but that's a partial amend for the botch I've made of my life with you. I'll try to make other amends to you later on. I don't know what else I can do now. I do love you, but know we can't live together."

He slumped at the table, sobbing. Gwyn was sobbing along with him. "Ky, it will be all right. You will know what to do. You've made a big start here already. You'll have a newer, better life. I'll always love and care for you."

She hugged him and rubbed his back. Ky hugged her tightly. "Jason's waiting outside with a cab. It will be all right."

Ky watched her walk across the patio until she went inside. She waved to him from the door. He felt better. Healing had begun.

Chapter Eight

"Is there anyone here who wants a white chip? Is there anyone here who is tired of the high cost of low living, and is willing to walk with us one day at a time?"

"I do."

Ky went forward to the rostrum of Amity, where Marta, an attractive blonde woman, handed him a chip.

"Tell us you name."

"I'm Ky, and I'm an alcoholic…"

Ky had awakened early that morning, his first day back in the Dual Cities. Around six, he went on his morning walk around Bowmar Estate. After breakfast, he looked at the file he had brought from Del Cara Hospital. He looked at the "after care" contract and its last provision: *I agree to attend ____ AA meetings during the first ninety (90) days of my recovery.*

At first, Ky entered "60" and then, upon reflection, crossed it out and put in "90."

At eight, he called the AA number he had found in the telephone book.

"My name is Ky, and I'm looking for an AA meeting."

A woman had answered, "There's a meeting at ten-thirty at Amity."

"I'm meeting with my lawyers at ten. When is the next meeting?"

"At 5:30, also at Amity."

"What is Amity? Is it a church? I need directions to get there."

"No, Amity is a clubhouse rented by the AA group. It's on Carlton Street, right behind Little Pigs Barbecue on Paul's Creek Parkway."

A little before ten, Ky arrived at Frank Folder's office on Freedom Street. He dreaded facing the music - a quartet of four malpractice suits. After a few minutes, Frank's secretary came into the waiting room.

"Mr. Gearan, you can go in now. Do you want coffee?"

"Yes, please, just a little cream."

Frank met him at the office door.

"How was your trip back?"

"Very smooth, hardly a cloud until we crossed the Mississippi."

"I have arranged for the sheriff to meet you in a few minutes to accept service of the complaints."

Frank's secretary brought the coffee. "The deputy is in the waiting room. Shall I send him in?"

"Yes, bring him in," Frank replied.

Ky recognized Deputy Dalton.

"Mr. Gearan, I hate to do this."

"That's okay. It comes with the job," said Ky. "I understand."

Ky signed the return of service and handed them back, and sat down to read the complaints.

"Read them carefully," Frank cautioned. "They're pretty much alike. They set out various acts of malpractice. Rogaire Tourain also added claims for sexual harassment."

"How could that be?" There is no employer-employee relationship here."

"Rog tried to cover all the bases. He can smell money in a case like a blind dog in a meat house. His former boss, Campbell O'Cam, taught him well. The sexual harassment claims are just window-dressing to inflame the jury. I'll make a motion to strike them."

Ky recalled an earlier encounter a client had had with Rogaire Tourain. The client, a woman, had given an affidavit over the phone to Tourain for a possible suit against Ky. When Tourain mailed the document to the client for her signature, she evidently had signed it without reading it first. After receiving a copy in the mail, she discovered that what she had told Tourain over the phone did not gibe with the signed copy. When she demanded that Tourain return the original document and he refused, she was forced to go to the state board, which compelled its return. So, thought Ky, that was his opponent in these cases.

Ky finished reading the complaint. "I can't believe what I've just read! Not much of any of this is true. How can he do this?"

"All Rog needs is word processor, the filing fee and few scruples. Each complaint standing alone amounts to very little, but by consolidating all four for trial, they will impress the jury. Repetition is a powerful tool. We can expect these plaintiffs to file grievances with the state board to put pressure on you to settle. Can you tell me what you remember about the incidents in the complaints?"

"In the first complaint, I remember putting my arm on the client's shoulder when I walked her to the door. She said and did nothing at the time. In the second case, I brushed my lips against her cheek when I opened the car door for her in the parking lot behind the office building. I remember going to the next client's apartment to interview her for the DWI case, as her driver's license had been suspended. I think I gave her a hug as I was leaving. In the last case, the complainant was visually impaired and the daughter of a client that I'd known for several years. I soon found out that she had counsel already for the cases she had called me about, and I left immediately. I did give her a hug at the door. I can't recall much else about them."

Frank got up from his chair and moved to the front of his desk. "Nowadays, you can't go around hugging clients. These hugs are going to be costly."

He looked directly at Ky. "You have to make a decision - settle now or fight these claims."

"I think we have to fight," said Ky. "What else can we do? I don't have much choice." He finished his coffee and put his cup on the table.

"Ky, you remember the answer to the question 'When to settle a case?'"

"Dr. Jackson said, 'Settle a case when it's cheaper to settle than to win the case.'"

"We'll keep our options open," said Frank. "The time to settle may come. I know these cases are going to be tough to defend. We have found out that picking a jury for a lawyer is about as hard as picking one for a building contractor or a used-car dealer."

"Has the profession's reputation fallen that low?" Ky asked, and then added, "Guess what I've done hasn't helped, and I feel guilty for my part in the loss of respect."

"Yeah, there's little respect left. We got to face the hard facts. We're like undertakers. Nobody wants us, but when they do, they need us real bad."

"What else can we expect from Rog? I didn't handle many civil cases in my practice - mostly criminal defense work, at least since leaving the trucking company."

Frank went back to his desk and took a sip of coffee.

"We'll be hit with Rog's full arsenal: motions, replies, interrogatories, requests for admissions, requests for production of documents, depositions, attachments, garnishments, freezing of your accounts - *ad infinitu*m and *ad nauseam*. You know the drill: 'No wrong without a remedy.' You have violated the lawyers First Commandment: 'Thou shaltcover thy ass (and thy neighbor's ass and his ox, too).'"

Ky got up and headed toward the door.

"What can we do to stop the newspaper from publishing these articles? They come out nearly every day. My mother, Gwyn and my children have been crushed. Gwyn has a tough election to fight."

"Not much, so long as they use the words 'allegations' and 'allegedly.' Since you are married to a judge, probably you'll be considered a quasi-public figure and the holding in the <u>Sullivan</u> case could apply to you. Even false statements are okay, if there is no actual malice."

"So, Frank, I'm fair game, and can expect that the reporter will continue writing articles, hashing and rehashing the events of my life, by pressing a button on the computer. Guess I'm powerless over this."

After the conference with Frank, Ky drove to Schneider Park, and spent an hour or two on the walking trail through the forest before returning to his mother's condo. The walk cleared his head.

Just before five, Ky walked into the Amity clubhouse. He looked around at the large open room. The worn sofa and chairs looked like vintage Goodwill. There were two long tables near the entrance. One was empty, and the other had ten or twelve people, all smoking and drinking coffee. It was like they described it at the treatment center. You can tell an AA meeting by the billows of tobacco smoke and steaming cups of coffee.

Ky was greeted warmly by those seated. He went to the coffee urn, drew himself a cup of coffee and sat down at the vacant table. Soon the crowd came in. Men and women wearing suits, others in working clothes. They got themselves coffee and took seats. They were laughing and joking. Ky was amazed. These people are happy and are having a good time. He began to lose some of his fear of not being accepted because of the media publicity. Soon, the room was filled with men and women of all ages, classes and races. Alcoholism was truly an equal opportunity disease; it was no respecter of people.

At 5:30, the meeting opened with the Serenity Prayer.

"Are there any newcomers to AA or visitors to Amity from other groups?" the chair asked. "Give us your first name, so we can welcome you."

"Yes, I'm Ky and I'm an alcoholic." The words came more easily than he expected. All around him the members welcomed him and shook his hand, and said they were glad he was there. Ky was grateful, as he was not welcome anywhere else. He thought back to a television documentary about chimpanzees in Africa. A lonely young female carrying a baby approached a troop of chimps. When the mother extended her had the other chimps accepted it - and began to pet the baby. Ky felt touched - accepted.

After he had received a white chip, the members joined hand and prayed, "Our Father...."

As he was about to leave, a tall man approached him.

"Ky, I'm Mac, and I've read about you in the papers."

The two laughed. They know about me, Ky thought, and it makes no difference. The ache in his middle began to dull and the hole began to close a little. Ky felt he had arrived at home.

In late May, Ky had enrolled in a master's degree program at University College - Glaston. It was now mid-August and he hadn't heard anything from the dean. Classes were scheduled to begin the middle of the next week. He spoke to Gwyn and Laurie Lea about his concerns. They assured everything was all set. Ky called the dean on several occasions, but he was unable to speak to him. The dean, the secretary had told Ky, was either "Out," "In conference," or "Leave your number, he'll call you back." Ky spent the rest of the week looking at apartments in Glaston. Fiona had suggested Eden Farm, which was just south of the city and easily accessible to the university. He arrived at the apartment complex around three on Friday and walked to the office. The building appeared to be a replica of Tara, columns and all. He halfway expected to be greeted by Miss Scarlett and Mr. Rhett, but was met instead by a tall, athletic redhead in a long blue skirt.

"Welcome to Eden Farms," she said. "I'm Tammy, your hostess-social director. You are just in time. One of our tenants has just vacated his apartment. I'll be glad to show it to you after we tour the facilities." They visited the gym, swimming pool, and the tennis, badminton, squash, handball, racquetball, paddleball and volleyball courts.

"The volleyball league season begins next week. We want you to join a team."

"Do I have to?"

"No, but let me encourage you to, as all of our tenants are young and active people. We have happy hour every Friday night and once a month we have dances.

Ky wondered if Eden Farms was a camp for Yuppies. Tammy showed him to the unit. It was upstairs, an efficiency, and barely adequate for his needs. They walked back to the office.

"When would you like to move in Mr. Gearan?" Tammy asked.

"Probably on Monday, but first I need to call the university.

"Help yourself to the phone. I'll get you a glass of iced tea."

"Thanks."

Ky finally got through to the dean. "Hello, Dean Vander Kiecke, this is Ky Gearan. You did get my messages? How about the fall term?"

"Mr. Gearan, your application has been administratively deactivated, but you may reapply for late admission."

Ky thanked the dean and hung up.

"Administratively deactivated?" he muttered. "This has got to be worse than being dead. If dead, one can be resurrected, but this? Deactivated? That's when a shell or bomb has fuse, primer and powder removed. The dean must have read the newspaper. The AP reports had gone to every paper in the state, including the Glaston *News and Record*. The Dean knows that I won't be able to get the letters of recommendation for the new application with my known track record, thanks to the *Daily* and the AP."

Tammy came in with the iced tea.

"Well, I won't be moving in on Monday."

"So sorry to hear that. We were looking forward to your being a part of the Eden Farm community.

Ky quickly got into his station wagon and fled - a fugitive from Eden.

When he returned to the Dual Cities that afternoon, he went to see Laurie Lea. She was on the patio near the pool. "What's up, dad?"

"I'm not in the master's program at Glaston - that's what's up. I've been 'administratively deactivated.'"

"Dad, that's blatant discrimination. They can't get away with that. You ought to sue them."

"No. I'm powerless to do anything now. Besides, I have Plan B. Wednesday, I contacted University College - Ardmont. They will let me take a few courses there this fall, and I can apply for their master's program in the spring. These are my kinds of folks - mountaineers. They're not like those snobs, those arrogant snobs in Glaston."

"Dad, where will you live?"

"I have talked to people at the Chamber of Commerce in Grey Eagle, which is only fifteen miles from Ardmont."

The next day, Ky drove 150 miles through the mountains to the town of Grey Eagle. He stopped at a local Exxon station and got directions to the Chamber.

"You turn raht at the stop light and go one block," the attendant informed him.

"Raht." That's "right," the dialect of Ky's childhood in Allister County. This dialect had always been soothing to him. His mother still had a trace of the flat "i" and even the Ulster "r." This was the dialect of the Scotch Irish. Ky had traced this dialect across several states into Texas, to Dallas and Fort Worth. The path of western migration could be followed by this dialect.

At the Chamber, the volunteer was helpful in finding him a condo on Highway 99, next to a horse ranch. This was a welcome change from all the bull in Glaston.

On the following day, Mitch went with him to rent a truck to move to Grey Eagle.

"Dad, I'll drive the truck. You and Laurie Lea can follow in your cars."

Ky was thankful that they were helping him move. Had it been only two months since the intervention and the trip to the treatment center? A lot had happened since.

For Ky's move, Gwyn helped them select furnishings of her mother's that had been stored in the garage - items her mother no longer needed since moving in at the end of April. Most of the furniture had been gifts from Gwyn. They had been a balm for the difficulties that existed between mother and daughter. Ky was often at the center of their contentious relationship - the battleground where they worked out their drama of guilt and resentment. Ky was glad that was all behind him and prayed that they would find peace.

The trip up the mountain was a welcome change from the August heat wave in the Dual Cities. The condo was gray shingled, trimmed with white, and built on one level. This made it easier to move the furniture. They finished unloading the van by late afternoon.

"How about dinner?" Ky suggested. "Pedro's is a couple of miles from here Mexican food is our family favorite, right?"

Mitch and Laurie Lea were willing and did justice to the buffet. Ky asked them to spend the night.

"We've got to get back," Mitch said. "We both start the fall term Monday."

"Okay," said Ky. "First things first."

Ky stood in the yard and watched the cars disappear down the mountain. He was alone - in exile. Had he not been "in exile" all his life? He recalled what a preacher had told him when he was a child, "We are but wayfaring strangers here…just passing through…Heaven is our home." Ky didn't know if it was good theology, but it described his aloneness and feelings of exile.

Chapter Nine

It was the first week in September, and Ky was in his condo at Grey Eagle reading a book assigned for his class at the university. The phone rang.

"Mr. Gearan, this is Edna, the secretary at St. Marks. We met at church Sunday before last."

"Oh, yes. I do remember you. What can I do for you?"

"Father Jim is out of town, but wants to see you when he returns. I don't want to talk more over the phone. Can you meet me for lunch at Sid's?"

"Yes, I'll meet you there in a few minutes."

Sid's was a converted gas station on Main Street. Ky met Edna a few minutes after one. She was seated on the terrace near the old gasoline pumps and the scallop-shaped sign.

"Thanks for coming. Thought I needed to tell you in person."

"What's happened?"

Edna stubbed out her cigarette, and said, "Yesterday, Father Jim received a manila envelope full of newspaper clippings about you. No note, no return address, but with a Glaston postmark. He was concerned about them, and asked me to call you. Can you tell what they are?"

"Edna, I haven't read them, but know in a general way their contents. Lawsuits have been filed against me, so I can't comment. I will, however, call him when he returns tomorrow."

After lunch Ky returned to his condo. When he met Edna, an attractive young widow, she impressed him. Now, he thought, she'll find out and shun me like other women do; no need to worry about it now. He wondered who could have sent these newspaper articles to Father Jim. Nobody knew he was attending St. Mark's. He had recognized no one in the congregation, and had introduced himself as only "Ky." He did remember meeting someone at that first Sunday. It was dedication Sunday for the newly renovated church. The Gunn family was being recognized for their gifts to the church: the stained-glass window with the Lion of St. Mark; the oriental carpet in front of the altar and the new maple pews. Ky sat near the front of the church. The Gunns had been asked to come forward for a presentation by Father Jim. An attractive young woman with brown hair looked directly at Ky and smiled. She came up to him after the service and introduced herself.

"Aren't you Ky Gearan? I'm Ann Flynn, formerly Gunn. I was an advisor to the young people at St. Barnabas and knew Fiona. I came up to be with my father and stepmother for the dedication. I'm married now and live near Glaston."

"Yes, I do remember. Fiona thought you were 'cool.' I know she and her friend Ellen were a trial for you."

"No, they were delightful, so lively and full of fun. They kept me from getting bored."

"Fiona is now married and living in Glaston. She would love to hear from you. Give her a call. She's in the phonebook under 'Devry.'"

"I will. Thanks for telling me."

After lunch with Edna, Ky called Fiona. She had not heard from Ann. He knew then that it had to have been Ann who sent the news clippings, and he wondered why she had done this to him. Perhaps, she thought the church should be a hotel for saints, rather than a hospital for sinners. The ache in the middle returned.

The next day he called St. Mark's.

"Edna, Ky. Is Father Jim in?"

"Yes, I'll connect you."

"Father Jim, Ky Gearan. Edna told me you wanted to talk to me. If it is about the newspaper articles, I can't discuss them because litigation is pending, and some of the litigants are clients."

"Yes, Ky, that's what I wanted to speak to you about, but I respect your position on them"

"I have thought long and hard and prayed about this, Father Jim, and feel that it is the Lord's will that I don't attend St.

Mark's. I really like the church and regret this, but when I go against the will of the Lord, disaster usually results for me."

"I appreciate what you have said. It is never wise for any of us to act against His will. Let me know whenever you need to talk to someone. I'm always available."

"Thanks, I will, Father Jim."

Ky was grateful for Father Jim's offer, but never called him again. He had become discouraged by what had happened at the church. This was the second time in the past few months that he felt forced to leave. He felt betrayed by people that he had known for a long time and who were fellow church members. He thought about the bitter experience that had made it necessary to leave St. Agnes. He had been a founding member and supporter of the church for most of his adult life. The rector, Jemmy, had been a participant in his intervention and had hugged him warmly when she left. The next Sunday she preached a sermon comparing the Daily stories to the "prophetic utterances" found in Holy Writ.

Gwyn had brought a copy of the sermon to the treatment center during Family Week. It was devastating - the loss of his wife and the loss of his church in the same week. At an AA meeting later, Ky talked to a minister-friend who knew his story.

"Ky, Jemmy was pressured by the feminists in the church to come out strong against you. It was a political decision, nothing personal."

"Like the 'Godfather'?"

"Yes, like the 'Godfather.'"

The sermon had damaged his cases. The jury pool had been polluted by Jemmy's actions. There was no way he could receive a fair trial in the Dual Cities, not with the *Daily* articles and the news of the sermon, and there was no way he could get a change of venue for trial in another county.

Ky felt betrayed by the feminists who had supported his House races for his position on issues they favored. He had donated legal services for their fundraising and had spoken publicly in support of their causes.

He recalled the communion service he attended in mid-August, in the chapel of Poteat University. At the service, Jemmy was the celebrant. Ky noticed she appeared nervous when she offered him the wafer. Father Fred and Chaplain Bill also assisted at the service. After communion, they all walked to the cafeteria for coffee. Ky tried to make small talk. He told Jemmy that he was going to take classes at University College - Ardmont, and was moving to Grey Eagle. Resentment welled up in him as he felt their relationship had been a dishonest one. He walked out with Jemmy to the parking lot. She paused at the door to her car, and there Ky told her of the harm her sermon had caused him. She reddened and stammered, "Forgive me."

Ky walked away without a word, he could not give her absolution. He drove away feeling sorrowful and the ache in his middle returned.

After the talk with Father Jim, Ky thought about moving away from Grey Eagle. Where could he go? He had signed a year's lease. He decided to stay until spring and perhaps pay a month's rent and be released. He began visiting other churches in the Ardmont area, but didn't join any of them. The hurt was still too great, and would take time to heal.

He visited the barbershop on Main Street in Grey Eagle. While there he talked to an old-timer. "Are you a native of Grey Eagle?"

"Yes, I was born here and have lived in the same house for eighty-one years."

"Can you tell me how Grey Eagle got is name?"

"Yes, the Cherokees gave this area its name. According to their legend, when a giant Grey Eagle visited the valley and flew over the mountains to the west, the Cherokee would leave the valley and be dispersed in the west. They were forced to leave here in the 1830s and went on the "trail of tears" to Arkansas Territory, now Oklahoma. A few escaped into the high mountains. The soldiers knew where many of them were, but did not pursue."

Ky thanked him and said, "Some of my Cherokee ancestors were among those escaping into the high mountains. I don't know much about them, but one was a medicine woman. Guess that's where I get my diabetes and alcoholism."

Ky wondered whether some of these ancestors had not lived here in the valley. He took, felt a sense of exile.

Ky stayed in Grey Eagle during the fall and winter, and moved to Ardmont at the end of March. He found a townhouse perched on the side of a mountain on the east side of town. It was a little smaller than the condo, but proved adequate to his needs. He hoped that this would be his last move, at least for a while.

The townhouse was only four miles from the university. He continued his literature and creative writing courses during the spring semester. In April, he applied for and was accepted in the master's program for the summer term. He enjoyed his classes and meeting other students interested in writing.

Ky attempted to meet members of the Ardmont Bar and attended a couple of their luncheon meetings. He didn't feel welcomed and stopped going. Now he had no more ties to the law, as the lawyers in the Dual Cities had dropped all association with him. Not one had called to ask how he was. He continued attending AA meetings in Ardmont. At noon, on most days, he attended the meeting at St. Lawrence's at Chad's Cove. At a meeting there, he saw Lori, who had been a member of the impaired lawyers committee with Ky. She greeted him warmly.

"Ky, we've missed you on the committee and wondered what had happened to you. Can you fill me in?"

"I'll be glad to. In mid-August of last year, I received a call from the director of the committee. He told me that I had been missed and wished me well. I offered to volunteer again, but was told that since I had relapsed, I wasn't eligible for a year. He suggested that I take a year's leave of absence, which I did."

"Gosh, Ky, that's too bad. Have you heard from any other members of the committee?"

"No, I haven't. You're the only one. Really wondered why I didn't hear from the local members. Guess I'm radioactive."

"Ky, you did break boundaries with clients and that has put people off. It'll take a while for them to accept you."

"Maybe never, Lori."

Chapter Ten

It was early Monday morning. Ky was just about to leave for the university library at the University when the phone rang. It was Dugald.

"Ky, your deposition has been set. It will be at ten on Friday morning, but you need to come by my office at four on Thursday afternoon to review what you're likely to be asked on Rog's deposition."

"Yes, I'll be there on Thursday. See you then."

Ky went by the library and returned a book, and then went to his English literature class - the Novels of Jane Austen. During class he was able to place all thoughts of the pending deposition out of his mind. He became more anxious during the week, and on the trip from Ardmont his anxiety increased. He arrived at Dugald's office a little before four.

The receptionist asked him to have a seat and said, "Mr. White will be with you shortly."

Ky was thumbing through a magazine in the waiting room when Dugald came in.

"Hope you had a good trip down. March can be a tricky month in the mountains. My wife's grandmother lives there. We try to visit in the summer and early fall."

"I had no weather problems. Not even the usual fog on Groundhog Mountain. I made good time today."

They went into Dugald's office. Ky noticed the usual clutter on the desk and the portrait of the Ohio Supreme Court with Dugald's grandfather, the chief justice, in the center. Dugald went over to a filing cabinet and got Ky's file.

"This file is getting fatter by the day."

"I'll brief you on what to expect. We have a protective order from Judge McLean. Rog wasn't able to quash our motion. This will restrict matters that Rog can inquire about. These are civil matters, but some may also be criminal; for example, assault. In these matters you can assert your Fifth Amendment rights and refuse to answer. Also, any matters involving clients of yours that are not parties to the lawsuits, the usual attorney-client privilege can be asserted.

"Also, Ky, on depositions, I don't usually interfere too much with the witness. I do this to get a feel of how he may behave on the witness stand at trial. Think of a bullfight. The matador sends the peons into to the ring to test the bull. Does he charge to the right or to the left, or straight ahead? Is he easily distracted by the cape work or does he charge at the matador?"

Ky understood this example. In a small village in Spain some twenty years earlier, he and Gwyn spent a Sunday afternoon with their tour group at a bullfight. At first Ky was fascinated by the pageantry - the trumpet calls, the entrance of the matador into the ring; the grace of the ballet-like movements of the matador; the swirling cape work, and everything up to the moment of the kill. He felt the stands shudder when the bull charged into the barrier, and was astonished when a bull picked up a horse and its rider with its horns, tossing them like a rag doll. He recalled the fifteen-year-old's first kill, but couldn't forget the piteous bellowing of the dying bull.

On the bus trip back to the hotel, Ky recalled Gwyn weeping and remembered the taste of the Manzanilla, the bullfighters' wine. He drank a whole bottle in an attempt to forget the reality of what he had seen. Ky had seen beyond the ceremony, the drama, the pageantry, and had seen it for what it was - a celebration of death. Vive la morte! Long live death! And now his case.

"You've chosen a good example, Dugald. I get the point. Many a time I've sat at a table with a frightened defendant - facing a jury who have all sworn to be impartial. We both knew that several of the jurors who couldn't wait to hammer the defendant. Is this my fate?"

"Remember, Ky, they can kill you, but after all its unlawful to eat you."

At that moment Ky failed to see much humor in Dugald's joke.

"Seriously, on the deposition: take your time; listen to the question; don't volunteer anything. If you don't understand the question, ask that it be repeated. I will always object when a question is improper. Above all, don't anticipate."

Ky left the conference feeling a little better. At ten the next morning Dugald and Ky were waiting in the library conference room of the law office. Law books lined the shelves from the floor to the ceiling. Dugald, Ky and the court reporter were seated at the large teak table in the center of the room. Rog arrived fifteen minutes late. Rog looked like a weasel, beady little eyes, like black-eyed peas, a pinched face with a sharp nose, but incongruously topped with a mop of carrot-color hair that looked artificial but was not.

Without a word of greeting, Rog opened his briefcase and began his examination. He led with what he thought was his strongest suite - the first newspaper article. "Mr. Gearan, have you read this article/"

"No."

"Do you want me to read it to you?"

"No."

"Well, Mr. Gearan, is this newspaper article true?"

"I don't know. I haven't read it."

Rog appeared flustered and put off stride by Ky's answers. He asked for the names and addresses of Ky's employees for the last five years, and the location and names of his banks and stockbrokers, with relevant account numbers. He inquired about the terms of Ky's separation agreement from Gwyn and the transfers of real and personal property.

"Mr. Gearan, tell me the terms of your mother's will?"

"I do not know, Mr. Tourain."

"You don't know much of anything, do you?"

Dugald objected loudly. "Stop badgering the witness!"

"I withdraw the question."

Rog then began to probe into matters covered by Judge McLean's protective order. Dugald objected. Rog responded angrily. "If that's what you're going to do, I might as well quit now and go back to Kilmont."

Rog tried again and asked similar questions. Dugald made the same objections. Rog threw down his file folder on the table. "That's it. This is over." He picked up his folder and brief case. He walked out of the room, slamming the door behind him.

"Ky, now you know what a son-of-a-bitch Rog is. Be thankful. He alienates everyone - witnesses, jurors and judges. He would be funny - he could be a stand-up comic of the insult school - if he weren't so destructive. He wreaks havoc in the lives of all those around him. When this case is over. I'd like to punch him just one time."

Ky turned to the court reporter. "Guess you didn't get many pages of transcript, and lost money on this job."

"Don't worry, I know Rog. Always I require a minimum amount plus mileage when I go out of town. Mr. White, will you want a copy of the transcript? It should be ready next week. I'll send it by express mail."

The court reporter picked up the equipment and left. It was 10:31 a.m.

Ky turned to Dugald. "What's the next step? Where do we go from here?"

"Rog will probably file a motion to dissolve Judge McLean's protective order. I feel it will be denied, as such order is discretionary with the judge, and he can't show any abuse of discretion here. We'll go to mediation in a couple of months. Ky, as you know, mediation is required in all civil actions in this state."

Ky knew that well. He was a trained mediator, having taken the training the prior January and receiving his license last May. Mediation shortens the litigation process, enabling the parties to assess strengths and weaknesses of their cases.

"I know, Dugald, too bad the process only works in about half the cases."

"That's too bad, Ky, because court time is the most expensive time and civil cases become backlogged because of the many drug cases being tried."

"You know, Dugald, that training course in Queen City is a good one. Two of my classmates were later appointed judge, one by the governor, to state superior court, and the other by the President, to federal district court. One of them is stationed in Ardmont. Guess I should go by to see him sometime, but discretion tells me not to."

"Discretion? Ky, it's been a while since you have exercised discretion. It isn't discretion that you've got here."

"Now, Dugald, don't rub it in. When can we expect to go to mediation?"

"Most likely in a month or two. Judge McLean always wants the parties to move their cases. 'Speedy trial' is his nickname. We'll pick a mediator from out of town. I don't want any of the local lawyers to mediate your case."

Ky did not think that mediation would work in his case. Rog wanted the last drop of blood, and wouldn't be amenable to a reasonable offer. He dreaded the process. He would have to confront Rog and his clients across the table.

About a month later, Dugald called Ky and told him that mediation was set for the week after Memorial Day. "Ky, we have a good mediator from King's County. He's an experienced trial lawyer and will do a good job here. We will be using the conference room of the Bartlett firm in the Kenilworth Building."

On the morning of the mediation, Ky went to a fast-food restaurant across the street from the Kenilworth Building. He ordered coffee at the counter and took a seat near the door. He looked across the room and saw Rog and his clients having coffee in a booth. They didn't see him, and he left. Ky finished his coffee in his car. He met Dugald in the lobby and told him what had happened.

"Ky, millions go there every day. Everybody has to be somewhere."

This relieved Ky's tenseness and he felt more relaxed as they entered the conference room. Rog soon came in with his clients. They all had bland, blank faces, except Eva Talbott. She was red of face, shaking like she had the chills, and adverted her eyes from Ky. He thought she didn't want to face him. That brushed kiss on the cheek would be costly for Ky, but Eva appeared to have some shame about her suit. Ky hoped that she wouldn't have a stroke in the conference room.

The plaintiffs had the opening statement as they were the moving parties and had the burden of proof. Not reasonable doubt, but the preponderance of the evidence.

Rog immediately went on the attack. He accused Dugald of bad faith in negotiations. He accused Ky of having made fraudulent transfers of property under the separation agreement. Rog blustered. "We think that we can reach that property and set the transfer aside, even though Mr. Gearan was very clever in the way be made these transfers."

Ky began to bristle at the accusation, but remembered the Serenity Prayer and calmed down. After Rog's outburst, the mediator recessed the hearing for a cooling-off period. Dugald was livid. "I just want to punch that little weasel one time - just one time."

Ky remained calm, accepting that settlement was not possible with Rog. Again he remembered the words of the prayer: "…things I cannot change…"

The mediator came into the room after meeting with Rog and his clients first. "Trying this lawsuit will hang out your client's dirty linen for all to see. This will amuse the public, but shame your client and his family and friends."

"Dirty linen?" Dugald was astounded. "This client has suffered weekly and sometimes daily airing of all his dirty linen in the media. This has gone on for months. What's left to reveal? What more can he lose? He has lost his wife, his family, his livelihood, most of his property, and every last bit of his reputation, his status, and prestige. Tell me, what's left?"

"Dugald, you know that jurors can be mighty generous with someone else's money. We've both been in cases where the recovery was massive, particularly where punitive damages are sought."

Dugald asked, "What has Rog offered?" He placed his legal pad on the table and prepared to take notes.

The mediator named a figure a few dollars less than Ky's remaining net worth. "Rog said he was being generous and would leave money for your client's retirement."

Dugald shouted, "Generous, hell! He's offered us nothing. We have to fight this case. Any counter-offer now is worthless."

"Very well, Dugald, we'll recess the hearing. If you and Rog can get closer in the future we can reconvene the hearing."

Ky and Dugald waited for Rog and his clients to clear the building, and then rode together down the elevator to the parking garage.

"How can you be so calm?" Dugald asked.

"I had no expectations. I had no expectations that we could settle with Rog."

Ky went by his mother's condo and visited her before returning to Ardmont. On the trip back, Ky kept repeating like a mantra silently, "No expectations - no resentments..."

Chapter Eleven

Ky had spent the night at his mother's in the Dual Cities. In the late afternoon he drove downtown to Dugald's office. He spoke to the receptionist. "I don't have an appointment. Is Mr. White in?"

"I'll check, Mr. Gearan. He's free. Go on in."

Dugald greeted Ky at the door. "What's going on?"

"Just wanted to say goodbye. I'm going to Ireland tomorrow."

"You're what?"

"Ireland. I'm going to the Gaeltacht - Connemara in County Galway. I will be taking an Irish language course. I need to get away for a few weeks."

"A few weeks? When are you coming back?"

"The middle of August. The fall term at the University College-Ardmont begins on the 20th of August."

"How can I get in touch with you? Your deposition with the state board will be set soon, perhaps in a month or two."

"I'll be staying with Brid O'Connally at Carraroe County Galway. I'll call when I arrive and give you the telephone number."

It was mid-July, the temperature and humidity both had been in the low 90's for the past several weeks in the Dual Cities. Ky was looking forward to being in a cool, green place. He always enjoyed visiting the Gaeltacht, the Gaelic-speaking area of Ireland and Scotland.

"I thought you could already speak Gaelic, Ky."

"I do speak a little Scots Gaelic, which is similar to the northern dialect in Ireland. This time I'll be studying the central dialect that's spoken in Connemara."

"Well, send me a postcard."

"I'll send you one with a greeting in Irish."

Ky drove to Atlanta the next day. Jason met him for lunch and took him to the airport for his flight to Shannon.

"Dad, have a good trip. See you in a month."

"This is the captain speaking, we are approaching Shannon Airport. Please fasten your seatbelts. Trays and seatbacks in the upright position."

The message was repeated in Irish. Ky could catch a word or two, but felt he needed lots of work. He knew just enough Scots Gaelic to be dangerous, as Irish had evolved since the end of the 16th century separately, while Scots Gaelic was the more archaic form of the language. Pronunciation had changed the most, and Irish had added lots more words.

After landing Ky went into the Irish customs area. He talked to a pleasant man and told him he had nothing to declare.

"Have a nice stay in Ireland, Mr. Gearan. Will you be looking up your roots?"

"'Fraid mine are in the Hebrides and in Antrim. They were Irish mixed with Vikings. I'm almost certain that some of my mother's people settled in County Carlow."

"So, you're both Orange and Green. That's a good mixture. Slan!"

"Slan!"

Ky did remember the word for goodbye. He had traveled much farther than the actual miles. He felt like a time traveler. These are the friendliest folks, he thought, just like those in Allister County fifty years ago. He was already glad that he had come. Ky left customs and went into the outer lobby, where be bought a bus ticket at the bus booth. His bus to Galway was to leave in an hour. He went into the snack bar and ordered a pot of tea and a scone.

"We call these biscuits back home in the states," Ky told the waitress. "This one tastes like the ones my Aunt Dot bakes. I'll bet this recipe has been handed down generation after generation for several hundred years and originated in Ireland."

"'Tis probably true. You've got an Irish face. Your folks must have come from here."

At nine, Ky boarded the bus to Galway. The first stop was at Bunratty Castle. The mists began to clear and Ky could see the cool green landscape from the bus window. At Ennis, the shire town, or county seat, the bus filled up with hikers from the States. They were headed for Galway and Aran Islands. It stopped at most towns and villages in Clare. The bus stopped at the inn in Ballyvaughn, where he and Gwyn had stayed five years before. This was the town of the Brehons - the judges. They got excellent service at the inn when Ky told them that Gwyn was a judge. He still had a picture somewhere of Gwyn standing next to a donkey cart. Regrets. Can't regret the past; be thankful for the years together.

The bus followed the curve of Galway Bay and Ky could see the Galway Hookers, ships with red sails. The regatta would be held in his village of Carraroe later on in July. The bus depot was at Eyre Square, a block-long expanse of green in the heart of the city. He caught a local bus there to the university. Ky walked through the gate to the old quad, a Neo-Gothic fortress built as public works during the potato famine. Two others were built at Cork and Belfast. They were called Queen's College then. Belfast is still named Queen's.

Ky marveled at the ivy on the towers and walls of the quad. He took a few pictures. The rest of the campus was, for the most part of a nondescript contemporary industrial style. Ky met with some of the other students and joined them in the cafeteria for a lunch of potato soup and tea. They were a varied group: half from the States, half from Europe, and two men from Australia. At two, they boarded the bus for Carraroe. It was a port on the bay about forty kilometers from the city.

Ky met his roommate, Liam, on the bus. The driver asked each student where he was staying and dropped them off there in town. Ky and Liam disembarked at Brid O'Connally's, about a mile from the Irish School. She greeted them warmly.

"I'm Brid, your bean-a-taigh, your landlady. A thousand welcomes to my home and to Connemara." Ky was amazed at her resemblance to his Aunt Amy, albeit a much younger version.

Ky met Dan and Ernie, who roomed across the hall. Ky began to wonder where Brid's family slept. There were six of them and three bedrooms. Guess they had to sleep doubled and tripled up. Brid treated them like family. She fed them potatoes and fresh vegetables from her kitchen garden. Sean, her husband, caught fresh fish from the bay, which was but a mile away. Last, but most important, there was hot water for showers.

Ky thought they had to be breathing the freshest air in Europe. It blew from the Pole across Greenland and Iceland and the Atlantic without anyone breathing it first.

On Saturday the students gathered at the Irish School. It consisted of two classroom buildings and a large green lawn surrounded by a rock wall. Classes were held Monday through Saturday, with a half-day on Wednesday. Ky and Liam opted for the beginners' class. Ky was surprised by the amount of vocabulary he knew, but had difficulty with the Connemara dialect. The "v" sounds in Scots Gaelic became "w" sounds. Ky liked the instructor, Michael O'Connelly. He was a poet and playwright. This was his last year at the school; next year he would be teaching at the University of Uppsala in Sweden.

Liam was tall with red hair and freckles; "Breac" (speckled) was his nickname. Liam was a good student. His aunt had been teaching him Irish since he was ten. He reminded Ky of himself at twenty-five. Liam ate no breakfast, had a snack at the pub and drank Guinness there some days, all afternoon. He would knock on the window around one in the morning; Ky would let him in; he would take a slug of *poteen* (like moonshine), go to bed, and was the only person Ky knew who snored lying on his stomach. He dropped out of school the last week and returned to the States.

Dan was in the intermediate class. He was a newspaper reporter from the Midwest who had burned out on the city beat. He was also in AA, and on walks from and to school, he and Ky shared their stories - their experience, strength and hope with each other. Ky believed that his Higher Power had supplied him with both "carrot and stick" - positive and negative examples for his life.

Ky got to know other students and enjoyed this association. He was particularly impressed with the grad students from Notre Dame. They kind of restored his faith in American youth. He met a woman from Wales and her daughter. She could converse with Cedric, a Breton student, in their common tongue. They sang together their national anthem. Ky was amazed that it was not "God Save the Queen" or "La Marseillaise." In fact, Cedric referred to "the French" as citizens of a foreign country. The month in Carraroe was working its magic. Slowly, healing was taking place. The tempo of life slowed down and life proceeded at a natural pace and rhythm. There was no sense of hurry, but there was always time enough - time enough to live, to be human, to pass the time of day with friends and strangers. Ky's worries and anxieties over his cases melted away. They assumed a different degree of importance. Now they seemed merely an annoyance, about like a button missing from his hip pocket.

Trying to learn Irish also helped. This difficult and arcane tongue had no single work for "yes" or "no." It had no real present tense. "Now" was just past or hadn't quite arrived yet. In a sense, the future was behind, instead of ahead, and would catch up to the now that never receded.

The Carraroe Regatta - the "Fete an Chara Rua" - was held on the third Saturday. There were two classes of races: the Galway "Hookers," sailing ships that were developed to carry peat to the Aran Isles and salted fish back; and the curraghs, similar to canoes, but longer and with oars. The curraghs were made of a wooden frame with tarred canvas stretched over it. Each village had teams of rowers and vied for the Connemara Cup. The season consisted of thirteen races, one each Saturday. Ky put on his bathing suit and waded in shallows while watching the races. The races were held at Coral Beach, the "Tra Doilinm." The beach was a fossil formation of coral and had gotten to Ireland by means of continental drift. There were three other beaches in the area, one of which had a ruined chapel and a graveyard next to the beach.

Ky and the other students cheered for Sean, the bus driver, for the Irish School. He was the favorite of the crowd and skippered the winning hooker. Sean and his crew had won seven of the eight races during the season.

The night before the races, Ky went to the fish fry at the Coral Beach. Mass was said for the safety of the racers. Guinness had a refrigerated van parked at the beach, dispensing both lager and stout. Ky had the foresight to bring a liter of drinking water, and ate the mackerel and mullet prepared by the women of the church. After the fish fry, Ky went back to Brid's. He watched TV and went to bed early. He woke from a dream, really a nightmare, around one in the morning. Ky had begun dreaming again while in Ireland. He mentioned this to his classmate Caitlin, a Notre Dame graduate, and she told him of similar experiences.

"Ky, I've begun to dream over here. Never do I dream at home. Is Ireland the land of dreams? Always heard it was New Orleans. They say we dream all the time, but just don't remember it. I have a friend who keeps a journal next to her bed and writes down the dream when she awakes. Think I'll start doing that."

Later, some of Ky's dreams turned into nightmares. They were about bad outcomes in his lawsuits. Many were worst-case scenarios. Ky felt that some law of reciprocity was working - peaceful and serene days - balanced by troubled nights where monsters were spawned. He feared these nightmares were premonitions. When his anxiety peaked he called Dugald.

"This is Ky. What's going on in the cases? I've been having bad dreams. Could they be premonitions of bad results?"

"Everything's about the same. Yesterday, I did get a notice of deposition from Karla Fenwick, counsel for the state board. It's set the day after Labor Day. We've got plenty of time to prepare. Are you scheduled to come home next Wednesday?

How about coming by office late Friday afternoon, say around four. So that's okay? See you then. Have a safe trip."

Ky felt a little better after talking to Dugald. He wondered if the medication his therapist had prescribed could be triggering these nightmares. He stopped taking the drug and in the a few days the dreams stopped. He felt a bit ashamed for thinking the dreams were bad vibes coming the state board or from Rog. Probably, just a chemical imbalance - not premonition of nemesis - not the furies - Karla Fenwick or Rog.

Ky took a bus from the village on Monday morning and went to the town of Ennis, near Shannon Airport. He had reservations for Monday night and Tuesday night at the Alba Lodge. The bus driver let him off in front of the lodge, which is the practice. Natural courtesy. Guess I'll miss this in the States, the thought.

On Monday night, he was asked to chair an AA meeting in Friary Hall, a space furnished by the Franciscans. Ky shared a brief version of his story, about ten minutes. The room was crowded. Alcoholism was a growth industry in Ireland, just like in the United States. Everyone shared and the meeting lasted an hour and a half. After the meeting, the AA secretary told the group that Ky sounded like Dolly Parton. Ky took that as a compliment. Always on trips abroad, he had lapsed into the dialect of the hill country, the flat "I," pronounced like "ah." Ky joined in the laughter. AA was alive and well and working fine in Ireland. For an hour or two, Ky was no longer lonely - he was among home folk - fellow AA's.

Early the next morning, Ky boarded the flight to Atlanta.

"The seatbelt light has been turned on. Seat trays and seat backs should be in their upright position. We will be landing in ten minutes at Hartsfield International Airport, serving Atlanta."

Ky was looking forward to seeing Jason and Dana again. They were to meet him in the international terminal. He cleared customs and walked toward the exit of the terminal. Jason was coming through the door.

"Dad, let me get your bag. I'm parked in the loading zone outside."

Ky got into the car. He thought Jason looked troubled. He appeared to be suffering from the loss of sleep and was not his usual upbeat self. He looked paler than usual for this time of the year.

"Jason, you were right on time. You got here just after I cleared customs. Thanks for picking me up. Is Dana working late?"

"No, dad. I didn't want to call you and tell you while you were in Ireland. Dana left me right after you left."

"Did I do anything to cause her to leave? Did all the bad publicity and my leaving your mother contribute to her leaving?"

"No, she came to me after work one day and told me that I wasn't 'meeting her needs.' She then suggested we separate. She called it a trial separation, but I know it's for keeps."

Jason, not 'meeting her needs? Jason had financed her master's of fine arts at the university and had taken her on a trip to Maui as a graduation present. He worked constantly in their yard. He had spent all of his money on her.

"Jason, what are you doing for yourself?"

"Dad, I'm increasing my therapy sessions and I have been going to AA meetings. Maybe you can go with me to one in the morning before going back to Ardmont."

Jason had begun therapy and attending AA after returning from Family Week at Ky's treatment center. There was no doubt that there was a genetic factor in Ky's and Jason's alcoholism. Jason was wise to try to get a handle on his alcoholism now while he was still young.

"I'll be glad to go with you. Except for the mini-meetings with Dan and chairing that meeting in Ennis I'm about a month behind and feel a little 'squirrelly.'"

They went to Cantina Palmona for dinner. It was at a shopping center near Jason's house. Ky loaded up on Mexican food and afterwards turned in early at Jason's.

At eight the next morning they were at the Early Bird AA meeting next to a liquor store near I-85. Ky had a lump in his throat when Jason shared, "I'm Jason, and I'm an alcoholic."

After the meeting, Ky hugged Jason and entered the ramp heading north to Ardmont. He thought about Jason. Ten years down the tubes. He could see his son giving up his power to Dana, a little bit every day. She was right; he couldn't meet her needs - he didn't have anything left to give. He wondered if anyone could. Possessiveness - that's the word. She had possessed him completely. She had well nigh destroyed his relationship with Jason, as she had with most of his friends. He's well rid of her, Ky thought.

Chapter Twelve

It was the second day after his return from Ireland. Ky had just finished breakfast in his townhouse in Ardmont when the phone rang.

"Mr. Gearan? This is Jay Ellsworth of Allister Braun, New York. We have received a writ of attachment and garnishment on your account. As of nine a.m. Eastern Standard Time, your brokerage account is frozen."

"Frozen! What do you mean frozen?"

"You will not be able to sell or buy securities, nor will you be able to withdraw funds, write checks or make deposits."

"Who signed the writ?"

"The writ was signed by a Judge Rutledge of the Superior Court in your state upon an affidavit made by an attorney, Rogaire Tourain."

Ky had a sinking feeling. More than half of his assets were in this brokerage account. He felt as if he had been kicked in the stomach. He thought, What else can happen? First, Dana leaving Jason, and now this. Then he remembered, trouble always comes in threes.

The telephone rang again. This time it was Hiram Upsom from Morrill and Company, Boston. He had the same message. This was the other half of his financial assets. Ky called Dugald.

"I got back to Ardmont yesterday afternoon. I've got writs on both brokerage accounts - everything is frozen. How can this be? These accounts total more than ninety percent of all my assets."

"Your brokers here in the Dual Cities have just faxed me copies of the writs. On their face, they seem to be in order."

"In order? This is financial ruin for me."

"Calm down, Ky. Can you meet me in my office at four today?"

"I'll be there."

Ky looked over the writs. "Dugald, this is a helluva a homecoming. Not two days back from Ireland and instant poverty. Because of my assets, albeit frozen, I can't qualify for food stamps or any other public assistance. More than ninety percent of my assets are tied up. Hell, I won't be able to pay your monthly statements, let alone my mortgage and car payments. What can be done about this?"

"Very little."

"Very little? There ought to be a law. What about the equitable principle of no wrong without a remedy?"

"It doesn't apply where the legislature has enacted a statute. All Rog had to do was convince a judge that you had fled or were about to flee the state, or were concealing your assets and hiding out within the state."

"Dugald, what if the stock market goes south. This will hurt Rog and his clients, too. Why would he do this?"

"Rog is not worried about that. He thinks you will fold and settle on his terms now. This is our dilemma. If we move to dissolve the writs and fail, and we probably will, then we will be in worse shape than before. The media will jump on this and prospective jurors will think that you not only harass innocent females, but also try to deprive them of just compensation for the wrongs done them. It's a lose-lose situation. The lesser of both evils is to do nothing about these writs. It's tough, but that's my best advice."

Ky hung his head and sighed, "You mean I've been screwed."

"Yeah, without a single kiss."

"Can't dwell on this, Ky. We need to talk about the state board deposition that's set for next week. One thing that you must understand is that Karla Fenwick is not out to find the truth, but to catch you in one lie. If you're caught, she'll jerk your law license immediately. Whatever you do - if you lose sight of this, you are history. Remember, there are no protections or privileges of any kind. There is no Fifth Amendment protection against self-incrimination, no right to remain silent, no right to

counsel in any meaningful way. This is the inquisition and Karla
is the Grand Inquisitor."

The deposition in the matter of Ky Gearan began at ten
o'clock as scheduled the day after Labor Day. Representing the
state board was Karla Fenwick, chief counsel. Representing Mr.
Gearan was Dugald White, Esquire, of the firm of Folder, White
& Freidbourg. Karla, like Rog, began the questioning with the
Daily articles.

"Mr. Gearan, have you read these articles?" Ky noticed that
she had reduced the articles so that they were impossible to read.
He thought, She doesn't expect me to say "yes" or offer to read
them to me. She has read my deposition and knows that I'll
reply, "no."

"No."

Karla didn't offer to read them to him or let him read them.

"Are they true?"

"I don't know, I haven't have read them."

"I don't know, I haven't read them."

Ky was glad now that he had decided not to ready any of the
articles. He wondered how much Karla knew. She had a stack
of material before her on the desk. She was a tall, slender
brunette, her straight hair pulled back from her face. She wore
no makeup and had a severe, serious expression on her face. Ky
felt a bit chilly. He knew now she was following Rog's script.
They're in cahoots. He thought she probably wouldn't pitch a
Rog-style tantrum, though.

"Very well, Mr. Gearan. Assuming that these articles are
true, does it not appear from the ages, backgrounds, class, race,
religion and national origins of the women that you were an
equal opportunity lecher?"

Dugald was furious, "Objection!"

"I withdraw the question. One more question about the
articles. Mr. Gearan, don't you find it remarkable that none of
the women with whom you allegedly had affairs has seen fit to
sue you or file grievances with the state board."

"No, I tried to be kind."

Ky did wonder why the four women with whom he had made clumsy passes had the gall to sue. All it takes is a greedy lawyer and a hungry client.

Karla began looking through the papers on the desk. She then began to ask specific questions about women clients. Ky answered the questions as fully and truthfully as he could. One client worried him - a woman named Nan Holcomb. Karla appeared to be reading from a report or a very long letter. Nan had been a client more than ten years ago. They had a brief affair, and their parting had been amicable. He was puzzled as to the relevance now.

"Mr. Gearan, do you know Nan Holcomb?"

"Yes, she was a client more than ten years ago."

"Did you have an affair with her while she was a client?"

"Yes, we had a brief affair. It was consensual."

Karla continued to question him about women clients. She must have access to all the court files of cases I've handled, Ky thought. It was now about one-thirty when Karla asked, "I only have a few more questions, Mr. White. Shall we continue or break for lunch now?"

"I'll defer to Mr. Gearan's wishes."

"Let's go ahead."

Ky wanted to get the questioning over with, as he was becoming fatigued at the grueling questions.

"Mr. Gearan, after all the trouble that you seemed to have with some of your women clients, you continued to have affairs or attempt affairs with them. Why?"

"Ms. Fenwick, I was suffering from the effects of untreated alcoholism. I had stopped drinking many years ago, but didn't seek treatment for my disease. I continued to do the same old things in the same old ways, expecting different results."

"Mr. Gearan, that sounds like a definition of insanity."

"Exactly."

"Mr. Gearan, you aren't trying to use insanity as defense, are you?"

"No, Ms. Fenwick. I'm just trying to explain the depth and source of my addiction."

"Oh, there is one other question concerning the newspaper articles. Mr. Gearan, you mentioned that the newspaper had slandered and libeled you. Do you mean to imply that you have a cause of action against them? If you do, why don't you sue them? Are you saying what they reported is untrue?"

Dugald jumped to his feet, "Objection! Please ask the witness one question at a time. I don't even understand the question and I'm sure that my client doesn't either."

"Mr. Gearan, you do understand the question, don't you?"

"Yes."

"Please answer."

"No, Ms. Fenwick, I agree that there is no cause of action, since the Sullivan decision requires that the paper have actual malice, even if what they report is untrue. My wife is a judge, a public figure, and most likely the holding in the case would extend to me also. Is it untrue? Certainly in most of what was reported. Truth as a defense? Perhaps the English rule should be followed: The greater the truth, the greater the slander."

"Mr. Gearan, thank you for your patience. You appear to have answered my questions, at least when you recalled the clients, as fully and completely as you could."

The deposition adjourned at one-fifty-one p.m. Ky felt no relief when Karla Fenwick left Dugald's office. To Ky, all doubts were now resolved. Karla would continue to pursue him until he was disbarred.

Chapter Thirteen

After leaving Dugald's office, Ky dropped by to see Laurie Lea. She greeted him at the door. "Hi, dad, how did the deposition go with Karla Fenwick?"

"It wasn't quite a disaster, but at least she must have thought that my answers were truthful. She was a bit frustrated at the fact that I hadn't read any of the newspaper articles, but questioned me about them anyway. Apparently she was following Rog's script."

"Dad, you probably did better that you thought you did. I hear mom's car in the driveway.

Ky got up to greet Gwyn. "You're early today. Did you have a small court docket?"

"Yes, thank goodness. This has been a tough week. How was your deposition?"

"Dugald seemed to think it went okay, but I don't know."

"Jason called today. Did he tell you about Dana leaving," Gwyn asked.

"Yes, he did. He seemed depressed that he couldn't make her happy. She never seemed satisfied."

Gwyn asked, "What's the next step on the grievances?"

"Dugald said a hearing would be set on the merits, perhaps in January. This will inquire into my ethical fitness to practice law. However, a hearing on his motion to dismiss the complaints will be set in October. If we win this motion, then your chances for reelection in November should improve. If we lose, who can say, but it will probably be detrimental to your success. Win or lose, an opportunity exists for the Daily to generate more articles, which won't help your campaign."

"Ky, do you know who the likely witnesses will be?"

"The four plaintiffs and perhaps several others. Karla Fenwick tried to extend her inquiry from the beginning of my practice. Dugald objected and got her to stipulate to a period of ten years since I returned to private practice. She asked questions about specific clients."

"Can you tell me who they are?"

"Can't tell you, as I'm bound by the Canons of Ethics as to confidentiality. I don't think you would know any of them, though. Karla will likely send out a press release when the hearing is set. No doubt she'll list the witnesses and tell what they will say."

Ky went by his mother's condo after leaving Laurie Lea and Gwyn. He ate a small snack there and drove back to Ardmont.

Chapter Fourteen

"Ky, Ron Taub, D.A.'s office in the Dual Cities. How are you?"

"Ron, I'm okay. What's up?"

"Ky, I've got some information for you. I've just found that Rogaire Tourain has visited my boss, Tim Marshall, and asked to lay a criminal information against you for sexual harassment, assault, and sexual battery. Tim refused. Otherwise, I could not tell you about it. This is what I've found out from Tim's secretary."

Ron was a close friend who was an assistant district attorney. He knew about Ky's malpractice cases and was using the D.A.'s office toll-free line to call Ky.

"Sheila says that Rog comes in like he owns the joint, presents his card and requests to see Tim. She ushered him into Tim's office. Through the open door, she could see Rog assessing the leather furniture, heard him mutter about the desk being like a baby flattop aircraft carrier. He went over and touched the pewter elephants flanking the State Code, picked up the picture of Tim with an old President with young hair, and picked up the picture of Tim with Governor Marrin at the victory rally. Tim came in about that time and, seeing Rog running his fingers over the polished top of the desk, said, 'Now about the furniture...it was a gift from my election committee.' Is Tim political or what?"

"She heard Rog begin the conversation, making small talk. 'I understand,' he said, 'that one of your former assistants will be running against Judge Gearan this time instead of against Judge Moore. Maybe, what I propose to ask you to do will help her chances in November.'

"Sheila said that Tim exploded. 'Never do I mix politics with the duties of my office. I do not discuss the activities of my former assistants, nor do I discuss why they are no longer on staff.'

"Rog had walked into a minefield, Ky. He couldn't have known the story of Tim's sensitivity about his former assistant. The comment was that, after she lost to Judge Moore, he had cut her off at the knees when he fired her. His only comment was, 'She serves at my pleasure, as do all my staff.' The facts are clear in that he did fire her that night. Ky, Sheila then told me she heard Rog's attempted apology. 'Mr. Marshall, I do apologize for bringing the subject up. I'm sorry.' Then Sheila heard Tom's reply. 'Apology accepted. Now, what can I do for you?'

"She said Rog asked Mr. Marshall to lay a criminal information against you before the grand jury. She then heard Tim ask, 'On what grounds?' Rog is to have replied, 'Sexual harassment, assault, and battery.'

"Then Sheila heard Tim tell him that sexual harassment was a civil matter and the other grounds were misdemeanors. He then asked Rog why his clients didn't file warrants for the misdemeanors. She said Rog replied that they wouldn't because it would look like they were doing so to force a civil settlement. Sheila saidTim really exploded. 'What?'

"I then walked in and heard Rog say, 'Sorry, Mr. Marshall. Just thought we could help each other out.' Tim was white with rage. 'Sorry? I've got three drive-by shootings that have been pending for more than a year and a backlog of drug cases. Sorry?' I saw Rog turn his tail and run."

"I recall Tim saying, 'What brass, the nerve of that ferret-faced lawyer trying to curry favor with me so that I'd do a number on Ky Gearan. Ron, he's got a hard enough row to hoe, what with the civil suits and grievances.' Then, he turned to me and asked if I remembered the way you had with a jury. I said, 'Tim, I tried Ky's last jury case. He had no defense, but used all the old warhorses of the law: reasonable doubt, probable cause, presumption of innocence, and so on. Tim, reasonable doubt....Ky could make a jury doubt that New York is a big city, or that the Pope is Catholic. I then asked him if he recalled that last case - State v. Reggie T. 'Ky's client shot the victim,

Denard J., from three feet with a .25-caliber automatic pistol, a Saturday Night Special. This bullet destroyed the breastbone, skittered around the rib cage and lodged near the spine. The doctor couldn't remove it for fear of paralysis. He might still become paralyzed. Tim, it would have been cheaper if the medics hadn't revived the victim on the way to the hospital. Now, the taxpayers are stuck with a $33,000 hospital bill. If he had not been revived, Ky's client would be facing murder one, as he robbed the victim after he shot him. The victim was conscious when the medics and officers arrived, and made a positive identification of the accused.'

"Tim wanted to know the results of the trial. 'Did Ky hang the jury? He asked. I told him, 'Yes. Eleven to one for conviction.' I thought Ky had found a Poteat University coed who wanted to be fair, who was hung up on the issue of intent. If the defendant intended to kill, this carried a penalty of twenty years rather than ten. She didn't believe the victim when he said he thought the defendant intended to kill him. The victim didn't help himself by smiling and acting unconcerned. I argued for ten minutes to the jury, and Ky no more than five. Afterwards, Ky said, 'I must have confused the jury for speaking such a long time. The jury was out for five and a half hours and was hopelessly deadlocked. Judge Craig declared a mistrial. I offered Ky a term of fifteen years, which the client accepted.'

"'Tim said, 'it will be a long time before the likes of Ky will be seen in the courts of this district. We will miss a worthy opponent and a friend. Sad to say, an era has ended.'"

Ky was gratified that his skills as a trial lawyer had been noticed by his peers and appreciated. He also felt regret that never again would use these skills in the courtroom.

"Ron, thank you for this information. Let me tell you what I found out later about the holdout juror. Last year, I was in an AA meeting and met the coed's father. I told him about he case and asked him to find out from his daughter how she voted. The next week I saw him again and he reported that she had voted guilty. All along, I thought it was the attractive gray-haired woman on the back row. Every time I mentioned our constitutional safeguards, her face lit up. Thank Tim for me and give him my best wishes."

"I will, Ky."

Chapter Fifteen

"Dad, there's an article on the first page of the second section of the Daily. The lead line reads. 'State Board Whitewashes Local Lawyer.' It purports to tell of what took place at the State Board Grievance Committee yesterday, and then rehashes your story. Do you want me to read it to you?"

"No, Laurie Lea. I have an appointment with Dugald this afternoon. I'll discuss it with him. You caught me as I was going out the door to come to the Dual Cities."

It was a beautiful fall morning. The leaves had completely turned in color at the higher elevations. Ky noted the changes in the colors as he traveled from four thousand feet at Ardmont to about nine hundred feet in the Dual Cities. Some of the trees there had not yet begun to turn.

Ky arrived at his mother's condo around noon. He was greeted with an offer to have lunch with her.

"Emma has fixed green beans, potato salad and fried okra. Gwyn has brought over the last ripe tomatoes from her garden and Emma has sliced them for lunch."

"Looks good and smells even better. Is that cornbread I smell in the oven?"

"Yes, Ky, it's Emma's secret recipe."

After lunch, Ky read a novel assigned in his literature course. At three, Ky went to Dugald's office. Dugald had moved upstairs.

"So, you've finally been kicked upstairs? Like your new office? What are you going to put on the shelves where Edwin had all his golf trophies?"

"I'll find something, maybe the odd law book or two. Champlain Title moved out to the Kenilworth Center to be near their clients. You don't golf, do you, Ky?"

"No, I discovered a great truth twenty years ago in a cornfield near the ninth hole at Oak Crest: Corn stalks are tougher than nine irons. I was powerless over golf and my game had become unmanageable. I didn't finish the back nine and haven't been on a course since."

"It's a pity you didn't find great truths in the case of other hobbies and pursuits, Ky. It would have saved you lots of money."

"Yes, and my marriage and profession, too."

"Ky, you have heard about the *Daily* article? They've got it wrong again. The hearing was on our Motion to Dismiss Grievances. There were six filed alleging various acts of ethical misconduct. The Grievance Committee dismissed outright three of them. They dismissed sexual harassment claims, as no employer-employee relationship existed, and all claims relating to sex with clients. They made a specific finding that this, standing alone, was not a breach of the rules in this state. Only if a conflict of interest occurred, such as representing a client that you were having sex with in a domestic case. None of that was alleged here. What is left amounts to no more than simple assaults. The paper wrote a good story, not a true one, when they alleged that the 'old boy network of the bar' was taking care of its own. We know you're not an 'old boy.' If you were, none of these claims would have been set for hearing."

"How did Karla Fenwick take it?"

"Not very well. She was shaking with anger. Karla made a motion for rehearing, which was denied."

"Dugald, when will a hearing be set on the merits of the claims?"

"Most likely after the first of the year. The committee meets again in January. Karla submitted a long list of witnesses that she plans to call. I found out that the board hired a private investigator from Glaston. He spent nearly six weeks at the courthouse here, looking through files, mainly juvenile cases you had handled. Evidently, he found little, as no juveniles or their guardians were listed as witnesses."

"How could he do that? Those files are confidential. They can't even be used in subsequent criminal cases against the juvenile when he becomes an adult."

"Ky, there are lots of things that have happened in your case that I don't understand. Take the list of witnesses that Karla submitted. Most were clients that you mentioned in the deposition, but others were not. I made a motion to limit the witnesses to be called to the ones submitted. This was denied. So the Lord only knows who she will parade across the stage. She has asked for a week for the hearing. Looks now that it will go into a second week. Happy New Year!"

"Dugald, we can expect that the *Daily* will cover this hearing with their usual flair for scandal. I don't know how much more my mother can take. Her nurses and maids try to keep the newspaper articles from her, but she hears it on the TV and radio and asks for the paper. Gwyn's election is in a couple of weeks. The reporter has written articles insinuating that she was complicit or at least aware of my escapades. One day she found him in her office snooping around, and chased him out."

"Yes, we are powerless over what the Daily publishes.

"What does Saul think of our chances at the hearing in January?"

"He thinks that you will receive only a reprimand or a short suspension from practice."

"How short a suspension?"

"He thinks no more than three months."

"Dugald, I don't plan to practice law again. No one would employ me. No clients would seek me out, and I couldn't expect to get liability insurance. I do have a mediator's license, and would like to do that. Probably, my loss of reputation among the Bar would prevent lawyers from using me, or surely their clients would object."

"Ky, stay in the day. Get out of the future. You are laying up for yourself wreckage of the future."

"Thanks for reminding me. One day at a time...."

Ky left Dugald's office and drove back to Ardmont. A few days later, he received a telephone call from Gwyn.

"Ky, I have just received a letter from Lucretia O'Fealiton, law professor at Poteat University. This letter was written on the law school's letterhead. It requests the Women's Attorneys Association consider filing an intervention in support of your disbarment before the grievance committee. I showed a copy of this letter to your mother. She is hurt and angry and is writing a letter to the dean protesting this action. Also, in the letter, she advises that she will make no gifts to them this year. She told me that she would never again give anything, and asked me to call you. Do you agree with her actions?"

"Yes! Hell yes! Not another dime, ever!"

Ky had been a loyal alumnus of both the law and business schools. He and members of his family had made substantial special gifts and annual gifts to both schools. He was an active participant in the annual and fundraising efforts and other programs of both schools. The total gifts would approach six figures annually. The university, in recognition of this, invited Gwyn and Ky to football and basketball games once a year, where they were guests in the president's box at the stadium. They were also invited to the schools' annual banquets, and were members of the Pro Bono Society, where the heavy-hitters of giving met twice a year. Ky was no longer invited to any university functions after the *Daily* articles appeared, but he continued to make annual gifts.

Several weeks later, Dean Lynch replied to Ky's mother's letter. He stated that he did not know beforehand of the professor's letter and, even if he had, he wouldn't have stopped it because of the principle of academic freedom. Ky felt they had gotten the old limp-wrist twist treatment from the dean: *I didn't know about it and, besides, I'm not responsible for the actions of my employees.* Most of all, Ky was angered by using academic freedom as an excuse. This doctrine only applied to what was taught in the classroom. His mother was infuriated by the dean's reply and wanted to write another letter. Ky advised against it.

"No need to get mad, mom. Now we'll have to be just before we are generous. Not one more dime to Poteat, not ever."

"Agreed, son, not another dime."

Ky called Dugald and told him of Dean Lynch's letter and what he and his mother had done.

"Good for you, Ky. I've long since stopped giving them money. Truly, at the law school, 'the right hand knoweth not what the left hand doeth.' Got some more good news for you, Ky. A letter came from the trial litigators. They are polling the membership to see if they want to intervene in support of your disbarment before the state board. They also attached a copy of a 'cover-thine-ass' press release, deploring your conduct and proposing a change in the rules of conduct that would prohibit sex between lawyer and client, except when the relationship already existed. Kinda takes care of the old boys, doesn't it? Probably, the change in the rule will be knows as The Gearan Amendment now and forever."

"Thanks a hell of a lot, Dugald. You really know how to cheer up a guy."

Ky was doubly depressed. First, the university and now the trial litigators. Ky had been a loyal member since returning to private practice. Not only did he support them with generous contributions, but also with his lobbying skills. Because of these skills, he helped the passage of several bills vital to their clients, and helped to prevent passage of ones that were detrimental.

Ky knew what to do. He attended an AA meeting of the Willingness Group. Ky was feeling depressed and powerless. Near the end of the meeting, he shared.

"I'm having a problem with acceptance today. Accepting things I cannot change. The game is nearly over and I have lost, but why does the full-court press continue?"

Adele, a young Poteat law student, was seated at his left. She lightly put her hand on his arm. She understood. His anxiety and depression dissolved at her touch. The AA miracle: a hand lightly placed, a word fitly spoken, and the whole world is changed. Adele understood.

Ky embraced Adele as she was leaving. "Thanks."
She smiled.

Chapter Sixteen

In early November, Ky received a telephone call from Laurie Lea. She was incensed.

"Dad, mom lost by two hundred votes. It's your fault!"

"It's not, Laurie Lea, it's not."

Ky thought, How close to the surface is the old me.

It was the morning after the election. Ky went downtown in Ardmont and bought a *Daily*. He checked the election returns precinct by precinct. One precinct stood out, Pleasantmont. Gwyn Gearan, 330 votes. Gwyn should have polled more than 700, Ky thought. He scanned the other precincts; the party and Gwyn's votes were about what they should be.

Ky began to beat up on himself. "Why was I so quick in answering Laurie Lea? I must make amends to her when I see her," he thought.

The next week he was driving to the Dual Cities. Ky was rehearsing what he would say to Laurie Lea. Probably the most truthful answer he could have made was, 'I don't know if what I did caused your mother to lose, but what I did didn't help."

He walked in Laurie Lea's home ready to make the speech he had rehearsed.

"Dad, we found where mom lost the election."

"Could it have been in the Pleasantmont precinct?"

"Yes, dad. It was there. How did you know?"

"I bought a newspaper and checked the totals, precinct by precinct. It appeared that the results were skewed in Pleasantmont. Why did she lose those votes there?"

"It was a registrar who worked for the senate candidate. He failed to turn in names to the board of elections. When voters came to vote on Election Day, some of them weren't eligible. Their names weren't on the book."

"Why did that happen?"

"Dad, we think that the registrar didn't get enough money or recognition or both for his efforts. It's a real shame..."

"Yes, it is. I do need to make amends to you, Laurie Lea, for my quick denial. My answer should have been, 'I don't know if I contributed to the loss, but my behavior didn't help.' Forgive me my denial."

"You're forgiven, dad."

"What are you mother's plans now?"

"The chief judge has appointed her as an emergency judge. She will fill in for absent judges throughout the state. Those that are sick, on vacation, or who have conflicts of interests. I think she'll also apply for the vacancy on the superior court bench. This is a 'woman's' seat. The governor is obliged to appoint a woman to the vacancy. There are several applicants for the seat. The governor generally gives first priority to judges who lose their elections."

"Let's hope she gets the seat. Being a judge has become important to her. At one time, I had some political clout and would have been able to call in some chips for the many favors I've done for the governor. Now my status is less than nothing. I hope I don't hurt your mother on this position, too."

"Dad, get off the pity pot. You always tell me not to turn your back on the past, for if you do you are bound to repeat the same mistakes."

"You're right, but knowing that I didn't directly contribute to Gwyn's loss doesn't make me feel much better."

Several months later, Gwyn interviewed for the vacancy. The governor offered her little encouragement, but didn't say she was out of the running. She felt that he thought that she might be too old for the job. Gwyn began to enjoy her work as emergency judge. She spent lots of time in Glaston. There, she could visit Fiona and Ken, and in times of bad weather spent the night at their home. Gwyn was assigned to hold court in Ardmont several times. Once, Ky joined her and the public defender for lunch at a downtown bistro. Gwyn soon gained a reputation for skillfully handling the "hot cases." They were considered "hot" because of local politics or kinship. Local judges couldn't, or wouldn't, handle these kinds of cases. Her election loss began to hurt less.

Chapter Seventeen

It was the week of Thanksgiving. A light snow had fallen in Ardmont. Ky had a telephone call from Dugald.

"Ky, got some news. This'll make your Thanksgiving truly thankful. Rog has lost his medical malpractice case."

"Didn't the jury bring back anything?"

"Zilch, zed, zero, nada, nothing. This is the break we've been looking for. Perhaps, he's now in financial straits. Think we should press for a settlement now?"

"Yes, I had given up hope after that mediation hearing. When can we discuss this further?"

"How about late this afternoon. Did you get much snow last night?"

"No, the roads are clear, Dugald. Will see you this afternoon."

There were a few patches of ice on Five-Mile Mountain, but nothing serious. Ky looked at the snow on the peaks of the ridge and felt grateful that some of his troubles may soon be over. Had it been a year and a half? It seemed longer. He arrived at Dugald's office a little after four and was ushered into Dugald's office.

"Are we going to settle these cases at last, Dugald?"

"Now's the time, if ever we are to settle. Don't think Rog has any other cases. Suggest that we now make an offer a little under what we offered at the mediation hearing. We can sweeten it later to about what we had previously offered. What are your thoughts?"

"Dugald, that amount is less that a third of what had been demanded by Rog."

"I know, but the difference is, he is a whole lot hungrier now than he was in May. I think we should make this offer."

"All right, I agree this is the time. Let me know what happens."

On Wednesday afternoon, Dugald called Ky at Ardmont.

"Ky, this is the best news. Rog will settle for the amount we discussed on Monday. He wants to get the money on Friday. I told him that he would have to release the attachments to the two brokerage accounts. After a little hesitation and after I told him that these accounts are the only sources of funds to pay him, he agreed to do so. He will meet with us at three on Friday afternoon at the offices of Morrill & Company. Think I'll ask Saul to go, as I might punch out his lights."

"That's a good idea, Dugald. I promise that I'll be on my best behavior. I confess I've had violent feelings toward Rog several times during the case. I'll call the brokers right now and instruct them to release the funds on Friday. Thanks again for all your efforts, and thanks be to God!"

A little before three on Friday, Ky arrived at the offices of Morrill & Company. As he was entering the door, he met Phil, a high school classmate who spoke.

"Hello, Ky, how's things? Are you still living in Grey Eagle?"

"Phil, I'm doing far better than I deserve. I have moved to Ardmont, but the newspaper thinks that I'm still in Grey Eagle. I would appreciate it if you'd not tell them I'm not still there."

"Don't worry, Ky. I don't have any love for the *Daily*. Not after the way they've treated you."

"Thanks, Phil."

In a few minutes, Saul arrived at the broker's office.

"Hi, Ky. It's long been a long road, hasn't it?"

"Yes, Saul, many's the day I thought we'd never get to this place."

"Let me give you the drill: Be pleasant and civil towards Rog, the son-of-a-bitch though he may be. I get along with him; I also loathe him. For some reason he seems to like me. I count that as an accomplishment, as Rog does not like anyone very much. You may make small talk, but not too much. Do not, I repeat, do not talk to the women. They're bad news and are strictly off limits. They are not and will not be your friends.

Consider yourself a goldfish for the next few minutes and that Morrill & Company is your bowl. Enough said?"

"Yes, you've made yourself perfectly clear, Saul. I'll comply."

About that time, Ky's former clients arrived in two cars. They were in an elevated mood, as well they should be. Wasn't this the big payday? Ky did not speak nor did Saul.

"What has happened to Rog? He should have been here fifteen minutes ago."

"He'll be along, Ky, and he'll have a good explanation for his lateness."

Rog arrived about half an hour late.

"Hello, Rog."

"Hello, Saul. I turned east at the Berwick interchange and then found I was headed toward Capital City. I then had to backtrack on Interstate 44. Also, there was construction around Glaston."

"There is always construction going on around Gaston," said Saul, "at least since I remember, and on Highway 421, before the interstate was built. Rog, are you still living on that farm down in Williams County?"

Ky had shared with Saul what Laurie Lea had told him about Rog.

"Yes, but it looks as if I'll probably move when I can afford it. My girlfriend is a big-city girl and doesn't like living in the country. She complains that the roosters wake her up, the odors are bad, and the muddy tracks that I call a road is impassable in the winter."

Guess he can afford to move now, Ky thought - if he has any money left after paying the note.

"Rog, did you go to college at Kilmont?" Saul asked.

"No, I went to Mulberry College at Mulberry, South Carolina, a small college in the midlands."

"I know where Mulberry is," said Ky. "When I was counsel for the trucking company, we had a terminal nearby. I think the athletic teams are called the Mulberry Indians or the Mulberry Braves."

"They were called the Indians, and at one time they had the longest losing streak in small-college history. Think it was sixty-seven games over an eight-year period. That was our claim to fame."

That was enough small talk for Ky. He remained silent for the rest of the time that Rog was there.

Saul continued, "Rog, you did get your law degree from University College-Kilmont, did you not?"

"Yes, I did, and I stayed there and was an associate of Campbell O'Cam. I began clerking for him at the end of the second year of law school."

Ky wondered what Rog would say if he knew that *he* knew he was still with Campbell O'Cam. So far, Ky had succeeded in being of "no mind." He had no feelings about Rog, either positive or negative. This seemed to have bothered Rog. He kept looking at Ky with a puzzled look. After all, Ky thought, it's only money...and that is all I am putting up...it is only stuff...and I have put little of myself in it.

"Saul did you get the certified checks for my clients and one for me?"

"Yes, I have them here. Did you bring the releases and judgments of non-suit with prejudice? Okay. I'll hand you these checks after your clients have signed all the documents."

Ky watched as the clients signed the documents. Saul gave the checks to Rog.

"Rog, do you represent any more clients? Wonder what we can expect."

"Saul, that is a confidential matter. I will agree not to file any suits against Mr. Gearan and further agree not to release any information about the settlement and its terms for a period of one week."

Rog and his clients left the broker's office. It was nearly five o'clock. Ky saw Rog on his car phone as he left the parking lot. He wondered if Rog was telling his banker that he had the money.

Ky shook Saul's hand.

"Thanks ever so much for what you and Dugald did in the settlement. I doubted we'd ever get to this point with Rog's personality and character defects. Did you find out when the grievance hearing will be set?"

"Our thanks to you, Ky. You are a super client. You did everything we told you and followed through promptly on each request. As to the hearing, Karla Fenwick has asked for a thirty-day delay. Probably digging up more witnesses. It looks like late February or early March."

"Saul, sometimes it helps to be compulsive. I never could let anything lie. I have to keep moving. Thank Dugald and Frank for me."

It was a few minutes after five, when Ky headed down the ramp and headed toward Ardmont. He felt little sense of ease. Rog was cagey about other clients, and Ky figured he would waste no time giving an exclusive to the Daily about the cases. After all, it was the Daily that had made these cases possible. Saul seemed to think that Rog had no more clients, but he agreed with Ky that Rog would notify the paper.

Ky began to relax and enjoy the golden glow of the late autumn sunset. It could have been worse...far worse.

Chapter Eighteen

On Monday after the settlement, Ky rushed to move his investments from his two brokers. He called them and instructed them to wire transfer funds to seven mutual funds. He could access these funds with an 800 number. With one phone call, he could withdraw or move his money. Rog's promise not to sue within one week was worthless, Ky believed. He transferred his townhouse in Ardmont to his children and requested that they put it on the market. He changed his telephone number after he had received a call from a Cy Breag, purporting to be from the Associated Press. He traced the call to a Capital City number. Ky thought it may be another private investigator hired by the state board.

Ky remembered an old saying: "Even a paranoid person has enemies." He then took the precaution of renting another post office box. Rog had also agreed not to announce the terms of the settlement for one week. On Tuesday, a *Daily* article appeared announcing the terms of the settlement, under the byline of Sean Tighman. This was it for Ky. He loaded his station wagon with some clothing, a folding cot, two folding chairs, a folding table, TV, radio, and his typewriter and drove south to the state line and the town of Tarleton. He rented a condo there, putting down two months' rent as a deposit, and paid one month's rent in advance. Feeling that he needed an out-of-state address, Ky went one mile south of the line to Ladium, South Carolina, a small town at the base of the ridge. There, he rented a post office box and filled out forms that he sent to the Ardmont post office giving them forwarding instructions for his mail. He then arranged for an unlisted telephone number. He gave the number only to Dugald, his mother, Gwyn and his children.

"Laurie Lea, I've moved to Tarleton. I am sending you a deed to the Ardmont townhouse, made out to all you kids. You can put it on the market. I want to be as fluid as possible, just in case."

"Just in case, what, dad?"

"In case I get some more lawsuits. The statute of limitations doesn't run out for another eighteen months, and that *Daily* article is likely to attract more suits."

"But dad, all this is crazy. You can't hide - at least as long as you stay in the state."

"Hindsight tells me I should have stayed overseas. You could have wired me some money and Gwyn could have transferred some of my assets. I panicked - I couldn't think straight at the time."

"Dad, did you consider that it wasn't meant for you to stay in Europe?"

"Yes, I think you are right. First, the railway strike and then the pickpockets. Guess that was providential. It was a good thing that I couldn't foresee the pain and the suffering of the last year and a half. Only had enough on my plate for each day at a time."

"Dad, this will never work, but I'll keep you informed of the happenings around here."

He was grateful. Laurie Lea was one in a million. He was glad that she was mainly in his corner because he would hate to have her against him.

The next morning Ky walked a couple of blocks into the village of Tarleton. He saw a historical marker in front of the Village Hall. It read:

Tarleton

Founded in 1790, by descendants of Loyalists. Named after Dragoon Colonel Banastre Tarleton, hero of the Battle of Camden, where he routed rebel militia. Ill, he missed the Battle of King's Mountain. Defeated at Battle of Cowpens, by militia under Daniel Morgan.

Erected by United Empire
Loyalist, 1905

About a block away Ky saw a café. He entered and was seated at the counter. The café was crowded with mainly retired folks.

"Welcome to the Charlton Café. What'll you have?"

"Oh, I'll have a cup of tea and an egg biscuit. Scramble the egg a bit soft. Thanks."

The elderly man seated to his left said, "You don't talk like one of them Midwesterners and certainly not like a canuck. Detect a faint trace of the hill dialect - say Wilson County. My name's Colonel Angus Thee. What's yours?"

"I'm Ky Gearan. Glad to meet you. 'Canuck' - haven't heard that term in years. Used to travel to Canada on business. A friend, who was an Ontario barrister, had the nickname "Captain Canuck." He used to try Provincial Transport cases and I retained him as local counsel. Are there any Canadians around here?"

"Lord, yes! They began coming here in the 1880's. Some of them tried to prove title to lands that were confiscated in the Revolution. Didn't succeed, but began buying up land. This was an impoverished area and land sold cheaply. They packed the village meeting in 1901 and voted to change the name of village from 'Lickskillet' to 'Tarleton.'"

"Weren't Tarleton's Dragoons the scourge of the countryside during the war? Didn't they loot, rape, murder and pillage the patriots?"

"Yes, and that's not all. The colonel himself boasted that he had 'killed more men and ravished more women than anyone else in the war.' He is supposed to have said this in front of respectable women when he went back to England. I think he rose in the ranks to lieutenant general - a rogue's reward. Some of his descendants live nearby, in the Woods' Colt Cove, but I imagine there's many more around. Be wary of folks with high foreheads and Roman noses. Like an Arabian stallion, he breeds true."

"Speaking of horses. I heard that this is horse country around here."

"Sure is. That's what attracted the Canucks here, along with the desire to recover ancestral lands. When they got here, one of the first things they did was to organize the Cornwall County hounds and brought in some Irish hunters. Real good stock. The hunt is still going strong after more than a century."

"Colonel Thee, I've enjoyed talking to you. You were close. I'm from Allister County, right across the Brushy Mountains from Wilson. Wilson County - that was a hotbed of Tories in the Revolution and of Union loyalists during the Civil War. My folks were patriots and Confederates."

Ky looked closely at the Colonel when he was leaving. Yes, a high forehead and a noble Roman nose.

Ky went into a mom and pop grocery and returned to the condo. He dialed the AA number in the telephone book. A pleasant-voiced woman answered. "Yes, this is AA. Meetings? There's one tonight at Bell's River Baptist Church and one Thursday at the Episcopal Church. You live across the street? Good, maybe I'll see you there Thursday. My name is Jan. Thanks for calling."

Around seven, Ky left the condo for the meeting at the Baptist church. About a mile out of town, he turned left on a gravel road that descended into a valley by hairpin switchbacks. He guessed he was lost. There were a few cabins, some of them log, built away from the road. At the bottom of the hill, he saw a sign: "Woods' Colt Cove." He turned around and went back up the switchbacks. While he didn't see anyone, he felt he was being watched. Ky didn't want to go there again.

At the paved road he took the right fork. After three or four miles, he saw a large white frame church with a few cars parked in the lot. No lights could be seen in the church, or in the building behind it. Ky parked his car and walked toward a small building - almost a shack - to the rear of the lot. He crossed a stream on a foot log, holding on to a rail suspended between two trees. It was nearly eight, when he opened the door to the hut.

Around a long table sat some members, mainly old-timers, drinking coffee and chatting.

"Good evening. I'm Ky. 'I was once lost but now am found.'"

Everyone laughed and greeted him.

"Ky, I'm Jed, the chair tonight. You must have turned off into the cove."

"Jed, I didn't see anyone, but felt I was being watched. It gave me a spooky feeling."

"It's not too bad. The Bannisters keep to themselves. They marry their cousins. Oh, they leave the cove to serve in the Army, retire and marry. They always come back. They distill good apple brandy from the trees growing in the western ridges. Some say the recipe was left by the aide to the Dragoon Colonel. Used to drink lots of it twenty years ago."

"Jed, do these folks have high foreheads and Roman noses?"

Jed laughed. "Been talking to Colonel Thee? Guess he's one of the few that got out of the cove and stayed out. He was orphaned at the age of five or six and was adopted by Major Thee, retired from the cavalry. The major sent him off to military school and then he got an appointment to West Point. He got the Silver Star leading a tank battalion at Colmar for General Patton's Third Army in World War II. He was wounded there but served later in Korea. Guess I'll start the meeting now."

Ky heard the comforting words and prayed the Serenity Prayer. He left feeling a little less lonely.

Early the next morning, there was a knock on Ky's door. It was the landlord.

"Mr. Gearan, would you mind moving to the unit downstairs. It is furnished and has two bedrooms and two baths. The rent will be the same. Sorry, I have to ask you to do this, but my daughter has flunked out of another school again. This time it was Mary Borden."

"No, I'll be glad to move. I could use a bit more room. I just have to fold up my cot, table and chairs and I'm ready.

Guess we have something in common. My younger daughter left Mary Borden at the end of her second year. After several other colleges and one university, she graduated. I was one proud dad, when she picked up her diploma. Maybe, it'll happen for you."

"I hope so, Mr. Gearan. Thanks for moving."

After the move, Ky went back to the Charlton Café. He looked around and didn't see the Colonel. He ordered breakfast and asked the counterman where the Colonel was today.

"Oh, the Colonel, his girlfriend lets him out only once or twice a week. She's a Bannister, too, about thirty or so years younger than he is. Supposed to be a second cousin, 'once removed.' Don't know about that 'removed' part. You've heard about the Bannisters?"

"Yes. The Colonel told me the folklore about them."

"It's not folklore. They don't marry outside the family. Some say the Colonel was shell-shocked in World War II or in Korea, but don't think so. It's that Tarleton mean streak coming out. That's what I think."

Ky went back to the condo after breakfast. He had a large living room and dining area. The best feature was the terrace with table and chairs. It overlooked the valley below and the beginning of the Piedmont scarp in South Carolina. To the right he could see Hogback Mountain and Ky marveled at how the leaves still clung to the ash and hickory trees even in early December. It was a good swap for the cramped efficiency upstairs.

On Sunday, Ky decided to go to eight o'clock communion at the Episcopal church across the street. He put on his new khaki slacks and plaid sports shirt, both gifts from Fiona and Ken. He entered the church. Everyone was dressed up. Men had coats and ties and women wore hats. Serving communion were a husband-and-wife team. She was the priest, he the deacon. Except for a young married couple and a pregnant woman, everyone else appeared older than Ky. "Retired military, corporate executives, and heirs with trust funds," he thought. "Definitely not my kind of place."

Ky stood outside the door after church but no one spoke to him. He went back across the street, feeling depressed. "I'll give it one more try," he decided. "I'll go the eleven o'clock next Sunday."

On Thursday evening, Ky returned to the Episcopal church for the AA meeting. It was in the boardroom. It was furnished with leather chairs and sofas, walnut tables, walnut parquet floors. Before the meeting he met Jan. She was a cheerful redhead of about fifty. Ky told her of his experience at church on Sunday.

"That's kinda the way they are. It's even worse at the small Episcopal chapel at the edge of town. 'God's frozen people,' someone called them. The name fits, she said."

It was a good AA meeting, as all of them were, though some were better than others.

Ky had yet to meet the landlord's daughter. She was never there during the day - at least she never appeared to be up. After dark, though, her convertible disappeared from its parking place. About two or three in the morning, Ky could hear her climb the stairs, turn on rock music, and then silence.

He went back to the Charlton Café during the week. He looked for Colonel Thee, but didn't see him. The counterman hadn't seen him, either. Ky's attempt to make conversation with the other patrons fell on stony ground and was met with silence - stony silence. Ky thought, "This town doesn't even have a McDonald's. I could always find conversation there. Do I really want to stay in this place?" He wondered.

On Sunday, Ky arose early. After his walk, he showered, shaved and dressed. He chose a pair of beige dress slacks, a blue blazer, a light-blue shirt, and his Clan Donald tie. Plain-toe shoes and dark socks completed his wardrobe. He was determined to try one more time at the church.

He arrived at eleven and took a seat near the front. The rector was celebrant. He was an older man with a neatly trimmed beard. During the announcements, the priest mentioned a coffee hour in the boardroom after the services. After the closing prayer, Ky went down the hall to the boardroom. He helped himself to a cup of lukewarm decaf tea. After a few sips, he put the cup down. He tried to make conversation, but received only monosyllabic replies. He quickly left the church and returned to the condo.

Ky packed up his few belongings and put them into the boot of his station wagon. After leaving a note for the landlord, he drove north toward Ardmont. He left Tarleton for good. At Henryville, he stopped at a fast-food place and had lunch. Around two, he drove into his driveway at the townhouse. Later he called Laurie Lea from a pay phone and told her what he had done.

Chapter Nineteen

On Monday, Ky went to the post office and picked up the mail. He rented another box and gave forwarding instructions for the mail in South Carolina. He called the telephone company and restored his phone service.

Among the mail was a plain brown envelope. Ky opened it and found Sean Tighman's article about the state board motions. He broke a cardinal rule and read it, thinking, "What's the difference, since I've settled the cases." A close reading of the article showed that, even though Dugald had won most of his motion, it was made to appear that he done so by underhanded means. Ky was glad that he had not read any of the earlier articles. The *Daily* used every opportunity to smear Ky. At every opportunity it spewed forth filth. Ky searched for the Latin word - vomitorium - that's the word for the *Daily*. It vomited its scurrilous garbage onto the public. Pandering to its lowest taste, constantly titillating it and whetting its appetite for scandal. The *Daily* set a standard for other newspapers; it was the "lowest common denominator."

In Ky's case, the *Daily* was continually playing a game of "gotcha." He remembered his grandmother telling of her father's capture inside the "Bloody Angle" after Pickett's Charge at Gettysburg. "He said, 'These Yankees bayoneted me in the shoulder and said, "We've gotcha."' I said, 'It's a helluva git that you've got.'" His grandmother said his great-grandfather's capture had saved his life. If he'd been left on the battlefield he would have died from his wounds, and if he'd survived, most of the company was later killed, and few were left to surrender at Appomattox.

Ky thought, "Yes, it is a helluva git the *Daily's* got. Has the wound and my surrender saved my life?"

When Ky returned to the townhouse he called Laurie Lea to tell her of his new phone number and mailing address.

"Glad you called, dad. Got some good news for you. Sean Tighman has been fired."

"Fired? How did you find out? A friend of mom who works in the business office of the *Daily* told her about it."

"Why?" What happened?"

"That article on the state grievance committee motion was his last one. The next Monday, he failed to come to work and didn't even call."

"Sounds like the Monday virus."

"Yes, seems like nicotine isn't his only addiction. He got a promotion and a raise after the first articles were written. Mom's source told her that soon thereafter, he began to come in late one or twice a week, but usually on Mondays or Fridays. He also failed to come on Monday one other time and was warned. The *Daily* has 'made him available to industry.'"

"Laurie Lea, I don't feel much elation at your news. They'll just find others to spew out their filth. I had a hard time with my resentments toward him. Used the AA method to remove them."

"How did you do that, dad?"

"I had to pray for the little son-of-a-bitch."

"How long did you have to do that, dad?"

"Until he was no longer a son-of-a-bitch. Seriously, my feelings of resentment and desire for revenge was eating my lunch. These feelings did not hurt him one whit, and they didn't stop him from writing articles. I finally got tired of allowing him to live rent-free in my head, and used prayer to evict him. It worked."

"Laurie Lea, a couple of weeks ago I had a message to call Cy Breag of the Associated Press. Have you seen any articles with his byline about me? They may say, 'Mr. Gearan was contacted' or 'Mr. Gearan was not able to be reached for comment.'"

"No, dad, are you sure he's what he said he is?"

"He could be another investigator hired by the state board to gather information about me. I can't think what else they could find. They have my deposition, the computer printout of all indigent fee cases for the last five years, and Rog's files available to them. Also, I have thought that it might be that bald photojournalist who tried to intercept me at the Capital City Airport when I returned from Paris. I think he is working freelance, but could be on special assignment for the Associated Press. It could be anybody wanting information about me. Heard a rumor that someone may be writing a book about me. Guess that's the price of celebrity - or notoriety.

"I'll be coming down there in a couple of days. I haven't started Christmas shopping. Your mother did all that for me. Ardmont stores are okay, but I think the selection would be better down there. I'll call you when I come into town."

"Okay, dad. I'll let you know if I see any articles by this Cy Breag."

Ky parked his car in the garage near Dugald's office. He stopped by and spoke to the receptionist and told her he would be at his mother's if Dugald or Saul needed to talk to him.

Ky discovered that the stores, with the exception of a few, had fled the downtown and were at the Winston Mall or the Expressway Shopping Center. It was lunchtime and he thought about going to a popular downtown eatery called the Horse's Mouth. Many professionals, including lawyers, frequented the spot. It was only a couple of blocks from the courthouse and, since it was near one o'clock, Ky thought he might see someone he knew. The restaurant was only one block from the *Daily's* offices and printing plant, but Sean Tighman no longer worked there.

Ky entered the cafe and looked around. He didn't recognize anyone at the tables or in the line and waited his turn to place in his order. The line was moving slowly today. After a few minutes, someone had gotten in line behind him. He thought he knew the voice. He glanced over his shoulder. It was Eldora Johns, the editor of the Daily. She was engrossed in conversation with a sales manager from the parent company in Richmond. Ky turned around at the counter. She looked directly at Ky, but gave no sign of having seen him. He placed his order, paid the counterman for the items, and went to any empty table near the rear of the restaurant. Ky wondered if he had become invisible. He thought of the radio play "The Shadow"; had he gained 'the power to cloud men's minds so that they could not see him?' Invisible? That's not so bad, mused Ky. A non-person? Wasn't that akin to bliss? To be free from the bonds of self - that artificial construct that he had dragged around all these years - that corpse - that body of death. Ky had been delivered without any effort of his own. Not by any conscious intent. Who is this person, this self that suffers? Who is he that experiences pain, sorrow, pleasure, joy? Ky knew, no it was beyond knowledge, that he was and was not that person, that self or not-self.

He knew again, that those who had intended him the maximum harm had succeeded in doing him the greatest good. That afternoon, on Fourth and Rowan streets, in the Dual Cities, deliverance had come. For a fleeting instant, he was beyond all good, all evil, all gain, all loss, beyond all honor and all dishonor.

"Thank you, Eldora Johns," was his silent prayer. Ky walked back to his car, with a sensation of floating, of lightness. What was this bliss? Grace happens.

Chapter Twenty

When Ky returned to Ardmont, he went out to the university. He met with his course advisor, who helped him select the two courses that he would take in the spring term. Ky explained to the advisor that the effects of the medication had dissipated, and that he would be able to continue his work in the spring.

He called Jason a couple of days before Christmas.

"Dad, here, are you coming up for Christmas?"

"Yes dad. I'll come up late this evening. Mom and the others are going to Mexico between Christmas and New Year's. Maybe we can do an AA meeting tomorrow. Does Amity still have the Alkathon?"

"Yes, we do. Let's shoot for the noon meeting on Christmas Eve."

Ky's spirits lifted a little. There was something special about an AA meeting with Jason. He was grateful. Ky recalled that Saturday morning in October, when Jason took him to the AA meeting near the Interstate in Atlanta. Jason had introduced him to some of the members and shared at the meeting. He felt that healing had begun in his relationship with Jason.

A little before twelve, Ky and Jason entered the Amity clubhouse. A Scotch pine Christmas tree stood in the corner near the speaker's podium. Other decorations were around the walls, and three tables laden with food were at the left rear of the room. Ky greeted the members and introduced Jason to them. He always would have affection for Amity, as it was there he picked up his white chip and began the journey "one day at a time."

Vincent was chair the first meeting. There would be meetings every other hour until midnight Christmas Day. Ky shared his gratitude and happiness that Jason was with him, that his children had not forsaken him, and that was because of the miracle of the AA program. Ky and Jason feasted on some of the food that the members brought and then they returned to Gwyn's.

Laurie Lea and Mitch were there. On the way back to his mother's, Ky began thinking of Fiona. He wished that he could see her over the holidays. It had been several months since he last saw her. She hadn't returned any of his phone calls or replied to his letters. He recalled the conversation with Ken last week. He asked why Fiona hadn't called or asked him over for a visit.

Ken had said, "Dad, she's been sick for most of the fall - a recurring virus and allergies that have been particularly bad in the dry weather - a drought, really. Dad, she hasn't recovered from what happened last year. There are constant reminders. Last week we were at a party at my Uncle Steve's house, and while there, a lawyer made a comment about your state board case. He didn't know that you were Fiona's father, and it hurt. Of course, the local newspaper carried the stories about you the day after they were reported in the *Daily*, and this hurts. I know she will see you when she is feeling better, dad. She does love you and it hurts her to see what is happening to you."

"Thank you, Ken, this does make me feel better."

Around two that day, Ky received an unexpected and welcomed phone call.

"Dad, Fiona. I would like to go to Christmas Eve services with you at St. Barnabas. Do you know the schedule?"

"Yes, Fiona, services are at three, five and eleven. Which do you prefer?"

"Five is fine with me. Will meet you around four at grandmother's house."

Ky began to get ready. This was the gift that he had been looking for - the magic of Christmas filled him with joy. He wore his red tie with Santa and his sleigh on it and put on his best dark blue suit. This was truly a gift - a Christmas miracle.

Fiona arrived a little after four. Jason was with her. They entered the crowded church together and found seats in the balcony. The trumpeter was playing familiar carols. Ky's heart and spirit soared. He wept tears of joy mixed with sadness. Fiona held his arm with tears in her eyes also.

Ky sang all the carols without a hymnbook. All the words had returned. Fiona shared his joy; with Ky she was transported to a place of peace and good will. A couple of his former colleagues smiled and shook his hand as they departed the church. This felt like acceptance.

"Dad, mom would like you to come over for dinner tonight. Jason and Mitch are helping her put on a Hawaiian feast. Ken is coming over about seven. We all want you to come."

"Yes, I'll be most happy to come."

Ky entered his former home a little after seven. It was decorated for the holidays. Delicious cooking smells pervaded the rooms.

He ate little of the food. Gwyn and the kids were sharing stories about the trips they had taken to Maui and to Mexico since Ky had left. This life was one that he had not shared. "What was left of his fatherhood and his part in the family?" he wondered. The answer was obvious. "Not much." This was what he had long feared: the sense of loss and the feeling of displacement were overwhelming.

Fiona asked, "Dad, you're not talking much. Are you sleepy? It's only nine o'clock."

"I reckon I'll get back over to mother's. I'll see you all there Christmas Day."

It was only two miles, but the trip to his mother's seemed to take forever. "Two miles and two years. Had it been that long?" he wondered. The time seemed both shorter and longer that that. Ky knew that his family had moved on with their lives, and that he was no longer part of any of it. Tears were blocked. He felt no relief from the overwhelming sadness, just the constant ache in the pit of his stomach.

Chapter Twenty-One

"Dad, thank you for the silver earrings. The design looks Celtic. Did you find them in Ireland?"

"Yes, Fiona, there was a shop across from the Irish Language School in Carraroe, where local crafts people sold their wares. I met some of them in the pub."

"Dad!"

"No, Laurie Lea, I didn't imbibe. Though at times I was tempted. You all know Guinness was my drink of choice. The music there was great. Some of my fellow students played instruments. The woman who wove your shawl, played the flute and tin whistle. Remember, there are only two social institutions in an Irish village - the pub and the church. One is expected to be in one on Sunday and the other during the week. This makes for great social cohesion and fellow feeling. We have lost this in our country."

"Son, is that where you got at that this beautiful silver cross?"

"Yes, the silversmith played the bodhran in the band."

"What's a bodhran?"

"Grandmother, I know what it is," said Fiona. Mickey Hart plays one. It's a hand-held drum. It's made of goatskin stretched over a wooden frame, much like those wooden cheese boxes granddad used to bring back from Canada."

Jason groaned, "Mickey Hart - the Grateful Dead, again."

"Don't knock them - that's where Fiona and I met. Mickey Hart's the greatest drummer I've ever heard," replied Ken.

"Thanks, dad, for this hand-tooled wallet. Mine is brown and Jason's is black. Were they made by a band member?"

"Yes, Mitch, he played the squeeze box, the concertina. He made his own bellows for the instrument."

About two, Gwyn and his children left his mother's home. They would be heading for the airport shortly for their trip to Mexico, to the Yucatan. Ky recalled one year when the kids were much younger, he and Gwyn had planned to go there. Ky bought travel books and maps. He also "pulled down the books" and got books from the public library about the Mayan ruins. Now, Gwyn was fulfilling that dream. Ky was grateful that they were going. He had partially recovered from his great sadness of Christmas. He went to an AA meeting at Amity. These meetings were godsends to suffering alcoholics. Ky thought, "Most of us don't take holidays very well, the sad memories of childhood - dashed hopes, drunken and abusive parents, sadness like Ky's, lost spouses and children. Perhaps, the greatest snare is "euphoric recall" - happy memories and the thought that a drink would help bring this back. Ky left the meeting feeling a whole lot better and less lonely. He remembered the slogan, "We are not alone."

Ky's mother was in bed when he returned; Christmas Day had worn her out. He fixed himself a light snack in the kitchen and made a call to his answering machine.

"Merry Christmas, Ky, hope you are having a happy holiday. Bobbie and I want you to come down to Port St. Helen for a visit. We've just finished our new house on the Sound. Give us a call."

It was Seth Layton. Ky recognized the voice. His former partner, always thinking of him. Ky had sent Seth a letter while he was in the treatment center. He wrote and called frequently. Ky's heart swelled with gratitude. He had recently married Bobbie, who had been his able assistant in his real estate business. Ky recalled those smiles she gave him in his darkest days. He would see her at early communion at St. Barnabas. Those smiles had helped keep him alive.

Ky picked up the phone.

"Bobbie? Happy holidays! Pretty good, kinda rough Christmas Eve, though. When can I come down? Is tomorrow too soon? No? I'll arrive about four or five. Church? The feast of St. Stephen, Deacon and Martyr? Yes, I'll be glad to go with you. Goodbye for now."

Ky hung up. He was elated. Truly, he was not alone. He felt grateful for all the people in his life. Somehow they always showed up when he needed them most. He felt blessed.

Ky packed his bag and loaded it into his station wagon before he went to bed. His mother was asleep. He thought he would tell her in the morning. She knew Seth and his parents. It would be okay.

After a breakfast of grapefruit, tea and oatmeal. Ky left the Dual Cities. Port St. Helen was a six or seven hour drive. He would avoid the interstates. They would be crowded with holiday traffic, particularly the North-South routes, from and to Florida. Seth and Bobbie lived on a sea island off the coast of South Carolina, near the state of Georgia. Savannah was the closet large city. He would "shun pike," stick to the blacktop highways through the swamps of the low country.

At first light, Ky left the Dual Cities. It was a holiday for most people. The streets were nearly empty. He drove through his old neighborhood and left town on Route 901. He followed this road through small towns, and villages until he reached the state line. He then traveled Highway 601. Near the state capital, he stopped at a truck plaza. The fill-up would last him for the rest of the trip. He turned east on 121, through the sand hills and then entered the low country of South Carolina. The car then turned south into a land of lakes and swamps. Ky saw a familiar sign from long ago, "Ten-Mile Swamp." He remembered the road, a ten-mile straight through the cypress swamp. The highway followed the bed of a railroad constructed by "Uncle Billy" Mahone, who had been Robert E. Lee's engineer. It was his men who built the pontoon bridge that enabled Lee's Army to escape intact, after Gettysburg. Much of the roadbed rested on rafts of submerged s\cypress logs. This technique was first perfected on the railroad laid through the Great Dismal Swamp of Virginia. During the ten-minute trip through the swamp, Ky marveled at the engineering feat. He also reflected that, were it not for Mahone's pontoon bridge, perhaps his great-grandfathers, who were in Lee's Army, might not have survived.

In a little over an hour after leaving the swamp, Ky approached Port St. Helen. He stopped at a service station to ask directions to the home of Seth and Bobbie. There was a customer at the counter talking to the attendant in a strange tongue. Ky heard the word "goobers" and saw the attendant hand the customer two sacks of boiled peanuts. This was Gullah. He hadn't heard this language since college. He recalled one of his professors from Charleston spoke the language, and learned that it was not English-based, but included words from several West African tongues. The only other word Ky recalled was "gumbo" - okra. So, Gullah was still spoken in the Sea Islands. Truly, Ky had come to a different place.

The customer left with his peanuts. Ky approached the counter.

"Pardon me, sir. I'm looking for an address on Moultrie Island. It's No. 18, Blue Heron Lane."

"Yes, go across the drawbridge and the causeway to the island. It's the first right on to Saltmarsh Road, then take the next right on to Blue Heron. You can't miss it."

"Thank you."

"Don't mention it. You're much obliged."

It was about three o'clock when Ky drove up the long curving drive to their home. Live oaks hung with Spanish moss were on the edge of the driveway. Azaleas were planted all over the yard. There was no grass, only sand. Ky thought that this would be a low-maintenance yard.

Bobbie and Seth came out to greet him.

"Welcome, Ky. You made pretty good time, must have been little traffic," said Seth.

"Yeah, there was little traffic, but I took my time - stopped a few times along the way. I followed your holiday route. Much better than the interstates. So scenic through the sand hills and the cypress swamps, and in the swamps I saw some hawks and maybe one eagle."

"You may have, Ky. The eagles are slowly coming back," said Bobbie.

147

"Let me take your bags," Seth said.

"No thanks, I've just the one. You know me, I always travel light."

Ky went into the house. It was all windows facing the marsh and the sound. Ky saw a lone sailboat in the distance. Water birds of all kinds were feeding in the marsh.

"Ky, you may take the guest room. It's off the library in the west wing. You still want to do communion at St. Helen's Church, don't you? We'll leave a little before six. Seth's going by the office. We'll meet him later at Jimmy's Acropolis Café."

"Thanks, Bobbie. I need to freshen up a bit anyway."

Ky entered the guest room had a view of the lighthouse on Huningdon Island about ten miles away. Beyond the light was the open Atlantic and east of there some five hundred miles was Bermuda. Ky reflected, Seth still the workaholic or, as he would say, "workophile." He recalled that Seth was not a churchgoer, but had begun going with Bobbie on special days. Ky took a shower, shaved and lay down a bit. He dozed dreaming about the trip through Ten-Mile Swamp.

A little before six, Bobbie brought her Jeep around the front of the house. Ky climbed up into the Jeep and they circled the house, spooking some birds in the marsh. They entered town on Bay Street, which ran along the waterfront. It looked like Nassau. Two- and three-story buildings with balconies and louvered windows shaded the sidewalks. They were painted in pastels, blues, yellows, and off-white.

The church was two blocks from Bay Street. It was in the center of a whole block. Huge live oaks and magnolia filled the yard. The church was whitewashed cut stone with a tall steeple that was a landmark for sailors along with Huningdon Light. Ky and Bobbie entered. It was all gleaming white inside; the pews elevated and with doors; clear, high arched windows covered by louvered shutters; at the arch shutters in the design of palmetto fans. The dark stained oak floors contrasted well with the whiteness of the interior. Ky looked the way they had come in.

He turned to Bobbie and whispered, "Where is the slave gallery?"

"There isn't one. I'll tell you about this later."

The celebrant began the service with the Collect for the Feast of St. Stephen, Deacon and Martyr. Ky understood the fitness of joining Christmas and the day after St. Stephen's death. Triumph and tragedy. Perhaps the reverse of his life - tragedy and then triumph. The paradox: surrender to win.

The Communion began. Ky knew the words by heart. The priest intoned, "Lift up your hearts!"

"The *sursum corda*." Ky recalled reciting the Mass in Latin when he was in high school. Though not Catholic, he was a scholar of Latin and learned the Mass. Funny how these memories had stayed with him, he thought. The congretation shouted, "Thanks be to God!"

Ky silently said, "*Missa est*." "The Mass is ended."

He followed Bobbie to the door, where she introduced him to Father Patrick, who was from Kenya. The Anglican Communion all over the world, wherever the Brits have gone," thought Ky.

"Now," Ky said to Bobby, "tell me about the slave gallery."

"Ky, this church was built in the 1830's after the first church burned. It was constructed of tabby, coral, shells and sand. The interior was all wood and that was what burned. We'll visit the ruins. It's south about two miles where the old town was. In this area there were two large plantations. First, indigo and rice were grown, and then the long-staple Sea Island cotton, which carried a premium price. The owners, having no other heirs, freed their slaves and left the land to them in their wills. Of course, in those days, some of the slaves were their children. This was in the late 18th century. Some of the descendants came to town and settled here. They were the artisan class: barbers, blacksmiths, livery stable owners, cord wainers, rope makers, sail makers, net makers, candle makers, carpenters, and cabinet makers. The finest cabinetmaker was John Elkin. I have a sideboard left to me by my maternal grandmother. He perfected the art of marrying magnolia veneers to poplar wood - light but with a beautiful grain. It's in our dining room at home.

"Almost forgot, why no slave gallery? There weren't many slaves here and both freedmen and slaves were welcomed to worship at this Episcopal church. This was a prosperous port with the revenues from export of the Sea Island cotton. Yields of cotton increased dramatically when freedmen began growing it - capitalism in its freest form - owner-workers. We have a few minutes, let's stroll along the ramparts.

"The ramparts were built after the War of 1812. They weren't of much use in the Civil War, as the Union Army had landed a few miles north and had attacked the town from the rear."

"That national cemetery on the edge of town, were those Union dead from that battle?"

"Most buried there were victims of the yellow fever epidemic of 1864-65. The slaves and freedmen nursed them, being immune at least in warm weather because of the sickle-cell trait. However, when the weather got cold many of them died, too."

They met Seth near the café and walked up the stairs to the "Acropolis." The restaurant was lavishly decorated with marine antique furniture and artifacts. One the wall facing the door was a huge framed deed - a land grant from Charles II to the Earl of Clarendon, one of Nine Lords Proprietors. It described a large area of land, extending "to the Southern ocean."

Seth said, "This means the Pacific. Some of us have been trying to get a group together to build a toll road to San Diego, but Jimmy won't sell!"

"Seth, haven't I done good? A fourteen-year-old who jumped ship in Charleston, washed dishes, ran hot dog stands, restaurants, bought apartment houses, and shopping centers?"

"Yeah, you done it all, by living over the store, working twenty-eight hours a day, and putting all your relatives to work, didn't you?"

"Seth, you know how to make a guy feel good! How about the crab soufflé and some *retsina*, with three glasses?"

"No glass for me, thanks," said Ky. "Been more than twenty years, but I did like *retsina*."

"Are you like me, a friend of Bill W? We meet at noon weekdays, across the street above the soda shop."

"I'll be there," replied Ky.

The crab soufflé was delicious. After dinner, coffee was served and Jimmy joined them for a cup.

"This is the land of opportunity, at least for me. I was a scared Greek kid who stowed away on a freighter bound for God knows where. The second day out I was discovered. This saved me from starving. They put me to work in the galley washing dishes. Soon as we put into Charleston, I jumped ship. Got a job in a Greek restaurant - washing dishes. Later, married the young widow of the owner. Still married after forty years - still washing dishes at home. Why did I leave Greece? This was after Word War II. Germans occupied us for several years. There were resistance groups, and my dad was killed by the Nazis. We lived in a small village in the mountains near Macedonia. Civil war broke out. For a while, the communists would occupy our village and they'd shoot all the fascists. When the fascists occupied the village, the opposite resulted. We learned to keep our mouths shut. Will never forget when I was sworn in as a citizen. Judge MacMilian said, 'Go, enjoy your freedom.' Nobody ever said that to me in Greece, the cradle of democracy."

"Jimmy, the moral of your story is, 'If you can't marry the boss' daughter, marry the boss' widow.'"

"Guess you're right, Seth, but if you do you are sentenced to a life of washing dishes."

They all left the restaurant in a good mood. "Why don't we drive down to Old Port late tomorrow afternoon and visit the ruins of old St. Helen's and then go to Uncle Clive's Oyster Roast?"

"Sounds like a winner to me. How about it, Ky?"

"I'm willing - seafood I love."

Early the next morning, Ky fixed himself a bagel and cup of tea. He drove to the beach on Huningdon Island. There was debris, fallen Palmetto trees, on the beach. Reminders of September's Hurricane Igor. The beach was washed away in spots. Lots of work left to restore it. He walked along the water's edge stepping over logs and debris. The beach was full of sand dollars that had washed ashore. Sand dollars - Oriente Island, sometimes knows as Sand Dollar Beach. He recalled his kids gathering sand dollars and trading among the kids from other beaches. Mitch was the "Sand Dollar King." He always found the most and always kept them, not trading any away. When asked, he'd say, "Just saving them."

At noon, Ky was at the AA meeting. Jimmy asked him to chair. He shared a short version of his story, and shared his gratitude at having friends like Bobbie and Seth, and now friends like Jimmy. The meeting closed with the words, "Who keeps us sober?" and the response, "Our Father..."

After the meeting, Ky and Bobbie drove to Old Port.

"Ky, if this were summer, we wouldn't be able to visit the ruins of old St. Helen or the church."

"Why so?"

"Just read the sign when we get there."

They pulled up to a parking space in the lot provided by the South Carolina Department of Archives and History. Ky got out and read the sign: *"Warning: this is the home of the mosquito and the red bug (chigger). It is not recommended that you visit this site from May through October. Old St. Helen was founded by French Huguenots, Sept. 10, 1670. The site was abandoned in 1734 because of 'varmints.' The present site of Port St. Helen dates from that time."*

They walked through the town and looked at the excavated cellars. They read the signs: "Jon Brevard House, c. 1681; Dram Shop, c, 1672; Apothecary Shop, 1679; Henri Beyle House, 1676," etc. The ruins of Old St. Helen's Church were impressive. Three of four walls were intact, but the roof was missing and the interior was gutted. A sign stated that it was built of tabby - "a building material composed of ground oyster shells, lime, and sand, mixed with sea water. Probably of West African origin."

At Uncle Clive's they stuffed themselves on bucket after bucket. Except for a few hush puppies and French fries, that's all they ate, washed down with sweetened iced tea with the lemons squeezed in.

Ky complained of feeling too full.

Seth said, "Oysters are like Chinese food - by bedtime you won't know you've eaten anything."

"Sure hope so, Seth, sure hope so."

"Tomorrow we'll visit my tea plantation," announced Seth.

"Tea plantation?"

"Yeah, Ky," Bobbie said. "Seth and four other investors are restoring a 19th-century tea plantation. It was abandoned during the Civil War and now Calhoun University horticulturalists are trying to restore the production."

"Calhoun University? Thought all they ran was a football factory."

Oh, Ky, you're just jealous because they regularly beat Buchanan and Poteat. Seriously, we hope to begin marketing by late spring. The brand name is 'Sea Island Tea.' The plantation is located on Trippe Island about twenty miles from here. I'll let you do some tasting of proposed tea blends."

About three in the afternoon of the next day they arrived at the tea plantation. They met the resident manager, who said that the original cuttings arrived from China in the 1830's. Remarkably, descendants of the original plants were producing tea leaves today. Ky went into the lab. He was handed cups labeled "A," "B," "C," and "D." He tasted them all and picked "D" as his favorite cup of hot tea. Then he tasted identical blends, now served as iced tea. Ky picked "C" as his favorite.

"Ky, you agree with us. We will pack and ship tea "C," as most Southerners drink their tea iced," the manager said.

"Seth, believe you have a winner here. My former partner - now a tea baron. Will you race ocean-going yachts? How does this sound: 'Sir Seth Layton'?"

"We're not issuing shares of stock yet, but we do have a small supermarket chain interested."

Bobbie picked up some fresh shrimp at the docks there. "We'll do barbecued shrimp tonight."

"That's Bobbie's specialty. She serves it with low country dirty rice."

They finished dinner with a piece of key lime pie rolled with graham crust.

"Bobbie, this is too much."

"Wait until you taste what I've got cooking for New Year's."

"'Fraid not, Bobbie. I promised my AA group in Ardmont I'd attend their party. First things first."

We are both sorry you can't make it, but know you have to keep your priorities straight."

Ky left the next morning and headed for Ardmont. The sadness of Christmas Eve had almost gone. He would face the new year with strength and hope.

Chapter Twenty-Two

"Ky, you are not leaving the party now are you? It's only a few minutes after ten."

"'Fraid so, Jan. It's getting close to my bedtime. First things first. This is my twenty-third New Year's Eve without a drink. When I quit drinking, I stopped partying and staying up to midnight on New Year's Eve. I found out the hard way that if I don't take care of myself first, I'm not going to be of much service to others."

"Sorry to see you leave before the dancing begins, Ky, but I understand. Happy New Year."

"And to you, Jan."

The AA New Year's Eve celebration in Ardmont began with a meeting at eight. The dance was to begin shortly.

At the meeting, Ky shared his gratitude for his higher power, the AA program, and the fellowship that had brought him safely through the year. He had risen early that morning. While on his morning walk, he began to review the events of the year. During the first part of the year, he was living in Grey Eagle and at the end of March moved to Ardmont. He took classes at the university during the spring term. In July, he had visited Ireland and took a course there in the Irish language. In his litigation, he was deposed by Rog and Karla Fenwick. In May, he had mediation in the lawsuits with no settlement made. In August, his brokerage accounts were frozen by Rog. Ky thought the biggest event of the past year was settling the malpractice cases. He had despaired of any settlement after Rog's performances at the deposition and mediation hearings. The new year would be the time to decide the course of the state board grievances. In a month or two, it would all be over.

On the day after the holidays, Ky visited the post office box. He had a notice of certified mail. The clerk handed him an envelope from Gwyn's lawyer. It was a divorce complaint and a return of service form. Ky read the complaint. He knew it was coming, but he again felt the ache in the pit of his stomach. Regrets. This didn't have to be. This was not a tragedy; he had every opportunity to change the outcome. He took the complaint and return of service to a notary public, signed it under oath, and mailed it back to the lawyer. Perhaps this would help Gwyn in getting that appointment to the Superior court bench. In another month, he would be free. He felt more unfree. Would he ever have a relationship? Would his reputation continue to follow him? It had here in Ardmont. His few attempts at starting a social life ended with excuses after a first date. Now he had stopped trying. This was the price for his folly.

The next week, Ky went to the university and enrolled for the spring semester. He felt that staying busy was the answer for him. Ky enjoyed the classes that he had there, and the association with fellow students had been a positive experience. What roots he had in Ardmont were at the university. He looked forward to seeing some of the other master's students that he had met there. Some had graduated in December, but he felt others would be in his classes.

Classes began the middle of January. He had chosen two, astronomy and cosmology, with Dr. Barber; and Jewish studies, with Rabbi Kravitz.

The astronomy and cosmology class was fulfilling an interest Ky had since he was a kid. Dr. Barber took the class outdoors to view the heavens on a regular basis. Ky's Cherokee friend, Ike Britton, was in the class, as was Shubra Kahn, a Hindu. Ky had met Ike two years before, and also his third wife, who was Irish. Ike was retired military, a member of Special Forces and of Delta Force. Ky had chosen as his term paper subject "The Cosmology of the Cherokee." Ike was invaluable in giving him insights on the subject. Ike had been born on the reservation and spoke no English until he went to school in the first grade.

Shubra was a new friend and gave Ky new knowledge of Hindu beliefs about nonviolence and non-clinging. She imparted to the class a Unitary perspective on the nature of reality. Ike invited Ky to the Green Corn Dance on the reservation. This gave Ky a new perspective on the nature of Native American spirituality. Perhaps the greatest new experience for Ky was the sweat lodge. This ceremony of purification served to clean out the dark corners of Ky's psyche and truly lifted his spirits.

In the Jewish studies course, Ky met Eva Havemeyer. She was Jewish and lived in Henryville. She commuted three days a week. She had an aunt who lived in Ardmont, the daughter of holocaust survivors. Ky had chosen "Children of Survivors" as the topic of his paper. Eva learned of this and introduced him to her aunt, who allowed Ky to interview her on several occasions. She was a pediatrician with a large practice. Ky used these interviews as the basis of his paper. Rabbi Kravitz invited the class to several services at Temple Emmanuel, including a Holocaust Remembrance. Ky discussed with the Rabbi the custom of Clan Donald to have yearly observance of the Massacre of Glencoe, an attempt of King William to exterminate the MacDonalds of Glencoe, an attempted genocide. Each year on February 2, Clan members gather and shout the word "Cominich" - "Remember."

The class viewed a film on the concentration camp at Terezin, known to the Germans as Tereseinstadt. The director of the film was a prisoner as a teenager and he appeared at the end of the film to answer questions about it. About five minutes after the film began a woman came in and sat next to Ky. He tried to bring her up to date on it.

"I know, I was there."

Before the film was over she was comforting Ky, who was weeping at the horrors depicted.

Later, Ky mentioned this to Rabbi Kravitz. He said he knew the woman, a retired psychiatrist from New York who lived in Henryville.

This was the best semester Ky had had at the school and the first when he was not preoccupied with his personal stuff.

Chapter Twenty-Three

On Friday afternoon, Ky left Ardmont for a visit with his mother in the Dual Cities.

"Anyone for brunch?"

"Count me in," said Ky. "I'm a bit hungry."

It was Saturday, and the meeting of the Willingness group of AA had just ended. Sometimes members of the group would gather at Harry's, a converted gas station, for brunch. Willingness had its meetings in the basement of a church next to Paul's Creek Parkway. This group had been helpful in his recovery. He shared his fears and anger at the newspaper articles, plaintiffs' lawyer, and feelings of loss of family. Perhaps the greatest thing about the group was that he had finally made friends with some of the members. He had not done so in the AA groups in Ardmont. It seemed that he was never included in lunch or dinner there, and going out for coffee was closed to him. Ky felt like this was partially his fault. During the first month in Ardmont, he went to lunch with some members of one AA group. They asked him things about himself. He made the mistake of telling too much of his story. Afterwards, he felt shunned by this group and others, as he felt the word about him had spread.

Ky had some acquaintances at the university, but not any he could call friends. Seldom did he lunch with any of them. For a while, on visits to the Dual Cities, Gwyn and some of the kids would join him for dinner. This ceased when they ran into a prominent member of the local bar at a restaurant. The next day he gave Gwyn a frown of disapproval at the courthouse. This ended the family dinners. Ky's social life in the Dual cities now consisted of AA meetings and early Communion at St. Barnabas on Sundays. He seemed powerless to do anything about his loneliness. On several occasions he had met women at AA meetings in the Dual Cities. At first, they seemed friendly, but always seemed to have other plans when he would ask them to lunch. They had heard his story. Truly, I am a social pariah, Ky thought.

Ky joined the group for brunch on that Saturday near the end of January. The remodeled gas station had a quaint charm. The food served by the Greek owner-manager-chef was delicious. Ky enjoyed coming here with the group, maybe once a month.

Ky's mother had moved into the house at No. 12 Essex Lane early last year. She bought it from the widow of a business associate of his father. His mother had visited the house on several occasions at parties given by these friends. She completely redecorated the house, spending thousands more than the purchase price. Ky's suite in the basement consisted of a large bedroom, bath, and den or sitting room. He had an outside entrance at the back of the house. He could come and go as he pleased without disturbing his mother.

Ky was grateful for all that his mother had done for him. She gave him shelter when the doors to his home and - indeed - all other doors had been closed to him. He recalled the cold winter nights as a child. His mother would put Ky and his older sister in bed with her. She would heat bricks in the open fireplace and wrap them in flannel to warm the cold sheets. He remembered how the wind whistled through every crack in the old house. He remembered his mother having to kill his pet chicken for Sunday dinner and getting sick after eating the drumstick. He never ate chicken again.

After they moved to town, Ky recalled his mother carrying him in her arms three blocks to the hospital emergency room after he was struck on the head by a rock thrown over the hedge in the side yard. Most of all, he remembered the day she sent him to the drugstore for spirits of ammonia to try to revive Cliff, a truck driver befriended by his father, who had succumbed to alcohol poisoning and pneumonia. Perhaps the greatest thing his mother did was revive Ky himself after an asthma attack. Ky remembered hitting the metal headboard of his bed when he was seven and summoning his mother from the front porch with his last bit of strength. Decades later, Ky enjoyed the use of his mother's complete office to type and copy his papers assigned in class.

The waitress came to their table to take their orders. She turned to Ky.

"What'll you have?"

"A cheese omelet, biscuits, tea, and Texas Pete hot sauce."

Ky always enjoyed the fluffy biscuits, and omelet with cheese and three eggs, which he liberally sprinkled with hot sauce made in the Dual Cities. "Pete" was actually a person, one of four partners in the business. He had been Ky's scoutmaster many years earlier.

Len and Rich, members of the AA group, were seated at the table with Ky. Rich was a newcomer, he had just picked up his red chip for ninety days of sobriety. He had had a minor accident and had flunked the Breathalyzer test. He went before Gwyn, who convicted him of driving while impaired. At first, he was very resentful, claiming he had been given a bad rap. Now he shared that this was the best thing that had happened to him. Rich was singing in a Little Theater production of "Evita."

"Rich, is this your last night in 'Evita'?" Ky asked.

Rich put down his coffee cup. "Yes, it's been a great run. Don't know when I've had more fun, and it's been good for me."

"I would really like to see you in it. Are there any tickets left?"

"It's a sellout, but you can go to the box office about one-half hour before the performance and stand in line. Usually some tickets are released right before show time."

After brunch, Ky went back to his mother's house, and after visiting with her he spent several hours in the office working on a paper for his Jewish studies class. Around five, he knocked off and went downstairs to his suite, where he showered and shaved. He kept some of his clothes in the closet in his bedroom. Ky selected a blue blazer, gray flannel slacks, light blue dress shirt, blue St. Andrew's Society tie, and plain-toed shoes with dark gray socks. Gotta look my best for the Artistic Elite, he thought.

Gwyn and he had been patrons of the arts. They supported the symphony, dance theater, opera, art galleries, and the Little Theater. They made generous contributions to the building of the present theater. Each year, they made substantial donations to the Arts Fund. Ky knew many members of the arts community. The director of the Little Theater was a close friend of Ky's younger sister. He was looking forward to seeing friends and acquaintances that he hadn't seen for nearly two years. He did fear they would reject him and not welcome him, but his expectations outweighed his fears.

Ky ate a light supper at his mother's, thinking that someone at the theater might invite him for dinner. In his heart, he knew that he was only hoping that they would, but his loneliness cried out for association with his fellows.

The Little Theater was near to Ky's mother's place. He left her driveway a little after seven. He was first in line at the box office. He thought that if any tickets were released, he'd surely get one.

A red-haired woman with two school-age daughters joined him in the line. She was friendly and greeted him warmly. "I've brought my daughters. They've been assigned to see 'Evita' at school." The woman introduced herself.

"I'm Sarah Benedict. We moved here from Colorado three months ago."

"I'm Ky, visiting here from Ardmont. I used to live here. My friend, Rich, is in the musical."

"Please tell me the part he plays. It will make it more enjoyable. It's been difficult for us to meet people here."

Ky turned to her and smiled. "Guess that's a dual cities' tradition. It's a hard place to break into, but an easy place to be shunned. If there aren't enough tickets, you may have mine."

"That's very nice of you, but there will probably be enough tickets."

Ky felt good Sarah's friendliness. There were enough tickets, and Ky and the two schoolgirls entered the theater together. In response to the girls' questions, Ky explained that

"Evita" was, indeed, a real person who had been the wife of a dictator in Argentina and was beloved by the "shirtless" ones - the masses.

Ky enjoyed the first act. Rich sang and played many parts, one of which was Che Guerva. He was elated and excited when he went into the lobby at intermission. Ky got in line and bought a soft drink. He came back into the main lobby and stood watching the crowd. He recognized many of them: the arts community, former churchmen, political associates, former neighbors, and law colleagues. None of them spoke or even indicated that they saw him. Ky was devastated. His elevated mood fell to the floor. He couldn't stand the obvious rejection and went outside into the street. Coming back inside, he met a trial lawyer at the door whom he had known for several years.

"Hello, Ky, how are you tonight?"

"Much better than I deserve, Ron. And you?"

"Very fine. My daughter Edna is singing in the chorus."

"Okay, I'll watch for her."

It was Ron Doyle, who was with one of the big silk-stocking law firms.

Ky was grateful. He thought, "gosh, I'm not invisible, after all. I may be anonymous, but that's not invisible."

After the musical, Ky drove slowly to his mother's house. Now he knew he could not expect to be accepted in the Dual Cities ever again. He had to scale down his expectations to zero. For he knew that unreasonable expectations were frozen resentments. Ky knew that any resentments were luxuries he could not afford. Not that they may lead him to a drink, but that they very well may lead him to non-sober behavior.

Chapter Twenty-Four

Ky was at his townhouse in Ardmont preparing for a class when Dugald called.

"Ky, I have some good news and some bad news for you. Which do you want first??"

"Dugald, give me the bad news first. First the poison and then the antidote."

"Okay. The Association of Women Attorneys voted to file an *amicus curiae* brief and have filed a motion to intervene in support of your disbarment. The one who filed the brief is your friend, Lucretia O'Fealiton, the president of the Association and law professor at Poteat University. I'll mail you a copy of the pleadings."

Ky recalled when Lucretia first came to the practice. She was employed by Legal Assistance. He had helped her try a case involving eviction of tenants from apartment. Although Ky was not directly involved in the case as a party, he did give her advice as to trial strategy and gave her information about cases to cite as authority. She won the case and received an award not only of treble damages, but also punitive damages. This was the first of several cases she was able to settle without trial, and each tenant was allowed to stay in his apartment and each received a cash award of at least one thousand dollars. Lucretia remained at the agency for another couple of years and then applied for a vacancy at the Poteat law school. Ky not only wrote a letter of recommendation, but also talked "off the record" with Dean Luych and several other tenured professors about her ability. She was later hired to teach landlord-tenant law. To her credit, she did support his campaigns for the state House of Representatives and enlisted the aid of the Women Attorneys and the local chapter of the National Organization of Women, where she was a board member.

"Don't forget the good news, Dugald."

"Yes. The Trial Litigators voted not to file an *amicus* brief and not to intervene to support your disbarment by the state board."

"Why so?"

"The official reason, given in a letter to Karla Fenwick, was that they were giving their support to a proposed rule that forbids sex between attorney and client unless same existed before the representation. I call this the 'Gearan Rule.'"

"Thanks a helluva lot, Dugald. What are you going to call the exception that protects those lawyers already having sex with their clients? Who can say when the relationship began? This protects the 'old boys.' They can have sex with clients, past clients, and future clients with impunity. Some of us lawyers are more equal than others. I can think of several bar presidents who were notorious womanizers."

"Ky, they didn't end up in the newspapers. You heard the saying, "That's what closed doors are for.' To be fair, this proviso, or grandfather clause, had to be placed in the proposed rule in order for it to have any chance of being adopted. It must be adopted by a majority vote of the board of governors, and those 'sexy senior citizens' won't vote for it otherwise."

Dugald, you mean 'dirty old men,' don't you? At least they refer to me as a 'dirty old man,' which is the politest term I've heard used about me."

"Ky, James Leceister VI, the president of the Trial Litigators, called me and told me of the decision before Karla Fenwick was notified. A committee had been studying this rule in the few states where it has been adopted without the grandfather clause. One of the states is Florida. The committee called some lawyers that they knew down there and asked them how the rule was working. The word they got back was 'nightmare.' The few cases that have been tried under this rule have led to endless litigation. Their hope is that the state Supreme Court will strike down the rule for vagueness, lack of standards, etc. James said that he argued against the adoption of the rule here. The consensus of the trial litigators was against his position. They were of the mind that because of all the publicity you had stirred up, they had to do something even if it was wrong. They felt like they had to cover their collective asses. That's what you said when you heard this."

"What did James say about the probability of the rule passing the board of governors?"

"He said that it would probably pass by a narrow margin. Maybe only one or two votes will decide and it would be likely that the chairman might break the tie. He said all the women members of the board were solidly in favor of the rule. Most of the men were against it, but with a few wavering souls. Cheer up, Ky. You wanted to leave your mark on the law. Everyone who reads the revised rule 7.1 will be reminded of Ky Gearan. Guess its popular name will be the Gearan Rule. Everybody is satisfied but you. The 'old boys' can continue having sex with their clients, the trial litigators will have covered their ass, and the public will be gulled, lulled again into a false sense of security. Your sin, Ky, was in getting caught. You have heard the politicians' First Commandment: 'Never get caught in bed with a dead woman or a live boy.' We'll change that for you: 'Never get caught making unsuccessful passes at lasses who are clients."

"Thanks again, Dugald, you do make me feel so much better. Will you mail me a copy of the trial litigators' letter and a copy of the brief and motion to intervene?"

"Sure will. Do you want me to send you the twenty-one newspaper articles and the five editorials that are appended to the brief?"

"Thanks, but no thanks, Dugald. What are the chances that the board will deny the motion to intervene?"

"Slim and none Ky. Remember, the state board grievance committee is made up of politicians. Their constituency is not the lawyers of this state, but the board of governors - the real 'old boys' who rule the legal roost in this state, the 'buzzards roost,' and they must keep them from becoming unhappy if they are to be reappointed. You are a media nightmare to the board.

They wish you had gone away. You told me about the train strike in England, being robbed on the Paris metro, and how you felt you couldn't stay overseas, but if you had these guys would be very happy."

In a couple of days, Ky received the brief and motion to intervene. The brief was a history of sexual harassment and sexual abuse. Much of it was totally irrelevant to Ky's case. He skipped over the parts that referred to specific newspaper articles. They had even included transcripts of tapes of radio and television news reports. Ky read the television transcripts, but had already heard the radio reports. He recalled with pain what he had heard on public radio. It was a report of a vote of the state branch of the National Organization of Women to seek disbarment.

He also remembered with shame what he did the next week. The public radio station was engaged in an on-air fundraising drive. He called in and told the volunteer that "he would never give another dime" to the radio station, which was sponsored by Poteat University. He felt doubly ashamed, because the news report had been put out by the state board and the reader could not have known about him. Besides, he thought, the station had been courageous in standing up to attempts by Poteat officials to censor and dictate program content. He resolved then, that he would continue to contribute anonymously to the station.

The motion to intervene was about what he thought. Essentially, it was a rehash, a boilerplate, of the main parts of the brief. Not many cases were cited and none from this state. There had been no cases ever tried in the state on this point, and the only cases cited were two from Florida and one from California. "California," Ky thought. "If I can't find a case anywhere else then I can always find one there." He had tried several times in trial and appeal briefs to argue points set out in California cases. The judge and the appellate court always ignored these cases.

Ky recalled what "Bud" Mallory, a specialist in appellate practice once told him, "There are fifty states in the nation and the fifty-first is California."

He felt that these California cases would not be ignored by the state board. Ky read on, getting more depressed at the recitation of the emotional harm done to the complainants. He stopped reading before the end of the motion, having gotten the gist of the pleading.

Ky began to regress into regrets over his conduct. How could he have been so foolish? His reckless behavior had led him here. The telephone rang; it was Laurie Lea.

"Hi, dad, you're in the *Daily* again today. Another story about you together with a rehash. Do you want me to read it to you?"

"No, I think I already know what it's about. Just read me the headline."

"Yes, here it is on page three of the second section: 'Women Attorneys File Brief and Motion to Disbar Ky Gearan; Trial Litigators Pass.' Is this what you thought it was, dad? I can read some more of it if you like. It's the usual rehash, plus this new material about the motion and brief."

"Thanks, that's enough. I know about this. I have just talked to Dugald. He has stopped telling me of these newspaper articles. You're taking the certified public account exam this week?"

"Yes, dad, I am. Wish me luck."

"Yes, I will even say a prayer."

Ky then read the letter from James Leceister VI. James really did not want to intervene. He has been a friend who has not deserted me, he thought. James had a practice that included representing lawyers before the state board grievance committee, and had been very successful in saving law licenses. He had not accepted any cases before the board and postponed those that he already had during his year's tenure. That's class, Ky thought. There had been a lawyer in the Capital Cities with the same name since the early 1800's. This was a legal dynasty like no other. Ky put down the letter, feeling a little better.

Chapter Twenty-Five

A few days later, Laurie Lea telephoned.

"Dad, here it is. This story is on the front page of the second section of the *Daily*. The headline reads: 'Disbarment Hearing Set March 17 for Ky Gearan; State May Move to Recover Indigent Fees.'"

"What's this about suing to recover indigent fees? How can they do that?"

"It says that on the cases where you allegedly had sex with indigent clients, the state contends that this was compensation, and you are not entitled to payment from the state for your services. It goes on to cite a state statute."

"I'd better call Dugald, Laurie Lea, and see what this is about. This is an outrage!"

Ky picked up the phone. He was boiling with rage. "This is Ky Gearan. Connect me with Dugald if he is available. He is? Thanks. Dugald, did you read the *Daily* article? How can they try to do this to this to me?"

"Yes, I did read it. In fact, I'm researching it now. There is a state statute that provides in cases where the state's agents, employees, officers, officials, and others get payment from a person or corporation, that said persons are not entitled to compensation from the state, and that the state can sue to recover this amount plus a penalty of twenty-five percent, plus eight percent interest. Also, there are some criminal sanctions in the statute. By this article, I think Karla Fenwick is creating more public sentiment against you. The article reads just like one of her press releases. Next time you are in town, call me and I will discuss my research with you."

"Okay, Dugald, but I think this is an outrage. I probably will be in the Dual Cities Thursday or Friday."

Ky thought, "There's no way the *Daily* and Karla Fenwick will give my story a rest. Just when I think things have quieted, another article or series of articles appears. When will this ever end?" he wondered.

Ky came back to town on Thursday afternoon. He called Dugald and arranged to meet him at five after he got out of court.

A little after five, Dugald came in from the courthouse.

"Come on into my office, Ky, I'll give you a report. The bottom line: 'Yes, Virginia, there is a Big Brother watching you.' This statute does say about what I told you on Tuesday. Also, I found few cases in which it had ever been used to recover monies. In fact, the last time it was used was more than five years ago. That time it was used on a county commissioner in Battenberg County, who had padded his expense account to the tune of about eight grand. As you know, Ky, there is no abatement statute in this state. Most states have such statutes that provide a law abates if it has not been used in twenty-five to thirty-five years. The honorable commissioner also paid a fine and got community service and a suspended sentence under the criminal provisions of the statute."

"Dugald, do you think the state board will do this to me?"

"Really don't know, Ky. If Karla Fenwick recommends this course of action to the state board and they accept it, then they will give it to the office of the courts to sue or to prosecute or both. How many clients are involved? How much money do you reckon it is?"

"I don't rightly know, Dugald. Not many clients are involved, and the fees are miserly in this district. The judges are famous for the meager fees that they set for indigent representation. Also, I haven't been paid for the last two or three cases that I handled last year - the last cases I handled before I retired."

"Have you followed up and filed a claim for payment of these fees?"

"No, I didn't want to rock the boat any more than I had to. There is only five hundred dollars or so involved here. I consider this amount is a farewell gift from me to the taxpayers of this state."

"Oh, Dugald, what about the phrase in the statute which states:...'already compensated my person or persons or corporation.' Is the state recognizing and condoning prostitution? In other words, recognizing payment in kind or barter for services rendered?"

"Yes, Ky, I think you have a point there. It would appear that if the state proceeds against you, it is sanctioning prostitution."

"Maybe, Dugald, the state is using a new definition of 'legal tender.' Some are more tender than others."

"I'm glad, Ky, that you haven't lost your sense of humor. We need to get together to discuss the state board grievance committee hearing. Saul should return next week from the case he has been trying over in Williams County. Call me on Wednesday and we'll set a time and a day to meet."

"Dugald, should I lose any sleep over the indigent fee recovery case?"

"No, Ky, sleep well."

"Oh, before I forget. I have drafted a letter to the editor of the <u>Daily</u>. I have no present plans to send it to them, unless you tell me otherwise. We have discussed in the past the futility of suing them for libel and invasion of privacy, but I still feel a need to let them know how I feel over what they have done to me and to me family. This is the letter:

> *To the Editor: Where can I go to get my reputation back? Where can I go to get the esteem of my family, my colleagues, my clients, and the public back? To what agency can I apply to get my reputation back? Where can I go without the tail of the <u>Daily</u> articles trailing behind me like cans tied to a dog's tail. Even discredited and disgraced officials of totalitarian countries can be and are rehabilitated after their deaths, and some during their lifetime after a change in regime. I make a modest proposal: Establish a department of restoration, not of buildings, but of people. Perhaps this could be funded*

by a tax on the media. A basic sin tax that would add a fraction of a cent to the cost of newspapers and to television programming costs for advertising. 'He who breaks must pay.' This, the oldest tenet of Anglo-Saxon law, applies to all, but not to the media. Break they do, with impunity, the reputations and they lives of those they trash. Sincerely, Kylemor Gearan.

"Ky, this is an absolutely great letter. Leave a copy for Saul. He will want to use this in his closing argument to the state board grievance committee. Particularly like that quote - 'He who breaks must pay.' The Daily has broken you - your law practice, esteem of colleagues, esteem of clients, and held you up to public scorn. Most of all they have broken the closest relationships of your life - wife and children."

Chapter Twenty-Six

It was Thursday morning, and Ky had spent a sleepless night. He thought of the telephone conversation with Dugald. Friday was decision day for the grievance committee. He would have to decide whether to go forward with the hearing or whether he should cut his losses and call a halt. The latter course would mean surrendering his law license. The appointment with Dugald and Saul was set for four on Friday afternoon.

Ky went to the university library to do some research on a paper for one of his courses. After an hour or two, he gave up and returned to his townhouse. He packed an overnight bag and drove down the mountain to his mother's place in the Dual Cities.

While driving, Ky went over in his mind what he knew, or thought he knew, about the testimony of the witnesses. He wondered if Karla would bring in a wild card witness who would blow him out of the water. A feeling of powerlessness swept over him. He began to accept this powerlessness. He turned on some Irish music on a FM station and soon thought no more about it. He knew that he was powerless, but not helpless.

Early Friday morning, Ky went by his former home to take Laurie Lea a book that she had wanted. Gwyn was there getting ready to go to Glaston for court. He told Laurie Lea of these thoughts about not going through with the state board hearing. She was furious.

"Mom, he's wimping out again!" she shouted.

Laurie Lea had been angry over the settlement that Ky had made with Rog. She had always been a fierce competitor. Laurie Lea had been a founding member of the women's soccer team at University College - Kilmont. After she graduated, the team won ten national championships, along with the World Cup and the Olympic gold medal. When she went to Germany, she continued to play the game. She was the only woman on the team of Iranian men. She would never give up anything, nor would she ever concede defeat.

Gwyn came into the room. Quietly, she ticked off reasons why Ky might consider contesting the state board case.

"Ky, Dugald came by my office a few days after the motion hearing in October. It was his contention, and I think it was correct, that under the present rules of professional conduct, nothing that the grievance complaints allege amounts to a violation of the rules. He further said that, had not the newspaper articles been so numerous, the committee would have dismissed all the grievance complaints summarily. As it was, three of the six complainants had all their claims dismissed, and of the remaining three only the simple assault charges remain. The worst-case result would be a short suspension and at the least only a letter of reprimand."

Ky listened closely to what Gwyn had said. He had relied on her good judgment during their years of marriage and knew that she was correct in this instance, at least in the legal sense. He could not tell her what witnesses might say, but beyond all that, the physical, mental, emotional and, yes, spiritual toll had been tremendous. He knew that he was nearing the end of his endurance. Ky also knew that Karla Fenwick would never give up. She would appeal any favorable ruling that Ky might get, just as she did in the Jamison case in Glaston. This case had been pending on appeal for nearly two years, with no end in sight. He had spent nearly all his monetary coin defending these cases so far. Did he have any emotional, physical, mental, and spiritual coin left to spend? Ky reflected on her words a moment more and replied,

"Yes, Gwyn, I do think you're right, but even a favorable ruling in the state board motion brought two more scurrilous articles from the <u>Daily</u>. We tried to keep them from mother, but she read them. Her blood pressure went through the roof and, along with it, her blood sugar. Mother thought, from the newspaper articles, that we had lost the motion. The fact was lost in the rehashing of all the bad allegations and new matter that had come out in the motion hearing. I'm sure that Karla Fenwick and Rog must have given the media a copy of the hearing transcript along with a carefully crafted press release. Karla has been relentless in her desire to have me disbarred. She has the limitless financial and personal resources to do the job and she will do it eventually.

"Also Gwyn, the continuing publicity will not help your chances of getting an appointment to the Superior court bench."

"Ky, let me worry about that."

"Gwyn, it's broke and I can't fix it," Ky said as he left the house.

On the way to Amity for the ten-thirty AA meeting, Ky thought some more about what Gwyn had said. "Am I cutting and running?" He intuitively knew his store of energy was nearly depleted, and most of all his psychic energy by these cases. Drip, drip, drip - a constant drain for nearly two years. Article, article, article, editorial, article, the newspaper spit them out in an unending stream. What profit would it be if he won these cases and lost the last bit of himself? He knew that Karla would appeal if she lost any part of these cases. Would he have the energy to endure for another two years? He thought not. The ache and the hole in the middle began to grow and grow.

At the end of the meeting, one of the Amity members read the Promises: "You will intuitively know what to do…and you will know peace."

Ky left with a feeling that he would know what to do and that would be the next right thing.

After lunch, Ky met with Dugald and Saul. Dugald reviewed the results of the motion hearing in October.

"In summation, Ky, very little remains of these cases, and what does is nothing serious."

"Dugald, you and Saul have done an excellent job for me. The settlement negotiations with Rog were a masterpiece of patience. I have no doubt that we can win these state board cases. I also have no doubt that Karla Fenwick will appeal. We need to stop the soap opera. When I see the pain and hear the sobs when my mother reads another article, and the pain and anger of Gwyn and Laurie Lea. When I know why Jason and Fiona don't call me, and why Mitch is never around, I know what's the right thing to do. I want Gwyn to get that Superior Court judgeship, and for my kids to have a relationship with me. Really, I'd rather give up the license now rather than later. My agony quota and that of my family has been filled and is overflowing.

"Ky." Saul spoke now. "We can readily win these cases and, in my experience, every lawyer who has given up his license has had regrets later. I know that you plan never to practice, but maybe out of ego, or prestige, or out of sheer personal satisfaction, you should reconsider your decision."

"Saul, probably your argument as to ego and prestige is the weakest one. It has no appeal for me. I have always tried not to define myself by what I do. Prestige and the trappings of the profession have meant little to me. I know they mean much to my mother, Gwyn, and perhaps some of my kids. I have tried to live my life without clinging to any notions of honor, prestige, status, success, and popular adulation. Since I could not cling to honor, now I cannot cling to dishonor. I must follow my intuition. Let the games end."

As he left their law offices, Ky was at peace. He had done the next right thing.

###

About the Author

Cé MacCiaran is a trial lawyer of more than thirty years experience -A.B Duke U. '52, JD Wake Forest Law '57, MBA Wake '82, and M.L.A. UNC Asheville, '01.

This book was written based on years of trial practice as prosecutor, defense lawyer and house counsel. The author has traveled extensively in Europe and the Caribbean. He is a divorced father of four grown children and is retired.